Indigenous Peoples for Black Lives Matter

An Injustice Anthology

Compiled by Jason Eaglespeaker

Eaglespeaker Publishing

Compiled, Edited and Published in a mere two weeks' time ... from June 5th, 2020 – June 19th, 2020 ... by hundreds of amazing Indigenous contributors ... and a Blackfoot guy named O'mahk'siik'iimi (Jason Eaglespeaker)

Contents

To everyone who's been beat by the cops.

Preface

My work is a rally ... my life is a protest.

Only a few short years after the **Occupation of Alcatraz**, the **Wounded Knee Incident** and the **Shootout at Pine Ridge Reservation**, a boy was conceived.

Today I am an Author, Illustrator, and Publisher of countless Indigenous authors from throughout North America and beyond. **Find everything at eaglespeaker.com**

I come from a long line of Indigenous peoples who have: stood up for their rights, educated others, peacefully protected (or what some call "protested"), overcome racial barriers, and did things few before them had done.

My mom, Linda Eaglespeaker, is Blackfoot. She is a Mo'toki - a Buffalo Woman. I have seen her sacrifice for our people first-hand - during our most sacred of ceremonies, the Sundance, and in everyday life, as I grew up on the Kainai rez (Blood Tribe). She endured relentless abuse as a child in residential schools, and yet still taught me to value education. She is selfless, she is my hero.

My mom's mom, Leona Eaglespeaker (Guardipee) is Blackfeet (Browning, Montana), she had 9 kids and lived to be 88 years old. She sacrificed everything for us. She taught me how to share my messages in a good way. She is the reason behind the "Elder Approved" logo on every single book I publish (she approved all my books early on, prior to publishing). My grandpa died in 1984, and my grandma passed in 2018, so for 34 years she was the last lifeblood of our family, she kept us all together, and she kept me coming home. She was my last blood grandma. Damn, I miss her.

My mom's dad, Glen Eaglespeaker, is Blackfoot. He was a famous artist – pen & inks, murals, giant paintings. I remember him painting me, too. As a baby, grandpa and grandma would take me often, back home to the Blood rez in Southern Alberta (I was born in Seattle). They practically raised me. Because of them, I grew up immersed in Blackfoot culture. From hunting, to prepping hides, to tanning hides, to cutting meat, to making stuff with the hides, to powwows, to ceremonies, to picking berries, to visiting peoples all over North America – it was daily life for me, not just on the weekends. My grandpa passed away in 1984. I was still really young, but he taught me so many things that gave me guidance as an adult. During our travels, he would tell me endless stories about the Blackfoot trickster – NAPI. Whenever I had a problem to figure out, he had a NAPI story to tell that helped me make sense of the world I was discovering. Today, I share those same lessons with people all over the world, in my NAPI kids' books.

My dad, Jeffrey Thomas, is Duwamish. Chief Seattle was Duwamish, and when they were forced to give up their lands for what became Seattle, the Duwamish people were adopted into neighboring tribes. My dad's tribe are the Muckleshoot (near Auburn, Washington). My dad is a Timber, Fish & Wildlife Biologist, and for as long as I can remember, he has been actively protecting our "cultural resources", from Mount Rainier all way to the mouth of the Puyallup River, and ensuring that all developers go through proper channels. Without people like him, many of our sacred spaces and areas of cultural significance would be simply developed over, and our fishing rights would be gone for good. My dad taught me to never stop fighting the good fight.

My dad's mom, Jeannie Thomas, is Duwamish and Warm Springs. She was a pioneer in Indigenous education back in the early days, the 60s and 70s, and even into the 90s. She founded one of the first powwow dance troupes in the Pacific Northwest, back when there were very few powwows. Even more amazing, she helped found the sadly defunct, "American Indian Heritage High School" - that thrived in West Seattle during the 1990s. When she passed away, I cut my long braids, to honor her memory.

My dad's grandma, June Courville/Siddle, is Duwamish. During an era when simply being Indigenous could be illegal, and very few opportunities were given to people of color, my great grandma created a chain of thriving taverns - the Pamona Tavern. She was also one of the first Indigenous women to buy a home, among her many other amazing accomplishments. I was fortunate to know her, I inherited her power, her drive, her business sense, and her kindness.

I could go on and on about my family's generational fight for what's right, each and every one of them endures the struggle, but let's jump to today, right now.

June 2020: we are in the middle of a global pandemic, peaceful protests against police brutality are happening nationwide, worldwide. Face masks are the new norm and we all meet online.

With a system clearly stacked against BIPOC (Black Indigenous People of Color), we share a common voice with our Black brothers and sisters against injustice. Like Dave Chappelle recently said, "The streets are talking."

"That's America!" you say, "We are all friendly here in Canada"

Indigenous people, from coast to coast, say, "Ummm, are you sure?"

The mandatory Canadian Residential School system was the opposite of friendly, but that's a whole other story, a whole other book series (HINT: this is where you google "UNeducation, Vol 1: A Residential School Graphic Novel" – all about my family's horrific experience in the notorious St. Paul's school in Southern Alberta. Find it here: https://www.eaglespeaker.com/uneducation-vol-one)

Let's get back to today. Check this out, between April 8th and June 12th, eight Indigenous people were killed by police, in Canada!

Let that soak in ... **EIGHT ... INDIGENOUS PEOPLE ... KILLED BY POLICE ... IN 'FRIENDLY' CANADA ... IN JUST 2 MONTHS**

Here is who they are (plenty details can be found online):

April 8, 2020

Eishia Hudson, 16, was shot and killed by Winnipeg police following a police chase, after a group of teens allegedly robbed a Liquor Mart in the city's Sage Creek neighborhood.

April 9, 2020 (less than 12 hours later, in the same city)

Jason Collins, 36, was shot early Thursday morning by officers who were responding to a domestic violence call.

April 18, 2020 (also in Winnipeg)

Stewart Kevin Andrews, 22, was shot by police after officers were responding to a report of a robbery, and windows being broken, in the Maples neighborhood of Winnipeg shortly after 4 a.m. A 16-year-old boy was also injured during the incident. Both were taken to the hospital, which is where Andrews died.

April 20, 2020

Everett Patrick, 42, was arrested on the morning of Sunday, April 12, after police responded to a report of a commercial alarm that had gone off at a business in downtown Prince George. Patrick was treated for injuries from the police dogs involved in his arrest. After release, he began having seizures and was returned to the hospital where he was found to have bleeding in his brain, requiring immediate surgery. He wasn't expected to survive. He passed away on the 20th, and his case is being investigated internally.

May 5, 2020

Abraham Natanine was murdered during an altercation with RCMP in Nunavut.

May 27, 2020

Regis Korchinski-Paquet, 29, died after her mother called for police assistance, after a domestic conflict with a request to take her daughter to the Centre for Addiction and Mental Health (CAMH). While her mother and brother were in the hallway of their apartment building, police entered the 24th floor apartment after Regis, who went to use the bathroom. The family heard Regis cry for help, followed by quiet, and then the officers confirming that she had fallen off the balcony. Regis fell to the ground below, and died at the scene. Her death inspired a number of protests in Canada against police involvement in her death and other issues of anti-Black and anti-Indigenous racism. These protests occurred at the same time as the George Floyd protests.

June 4, 2020

Chantal Moore, 26, was shot and killed by police in Edmundston, New Brunswick during a wellness check. A wave of protests followed.

June 12, 2020

Rodney Levi, 48. The RCMP said in a June 13 statement that it received a call Friday about an "unwanted person" at a home near Metepenagiag First Nation, New Brunswick. The RCMP claims that officers were met with a man carrying knives once they arrived on scene, and that several attempts to subdue him with a stun gun failed. That's when an RCMP officer shot Levi, who was taken to hospital. He was declared dead later that night.

Sadly, we will hear of more stories like this.

The goal of this book is to give voice to the voiceless, to offer a glimpse into the endless injustices that North America's Indigenous peoples endure on a daily basis, here and now. Contributors are from tribes coast to coast, and north to south, there are no areas immune to injustice.

If you are a non-BIPOC reader, some of these uncensored real life experiences will rock your foundations, they may even seem far -fetched or unbelievable. All this passion and pain and prejudice, and you might even be tempted to say, "can't we just focus on the positives?" or "if you weren't so angry, your message would come across better". If you ever feel that way, stop yourself immediately and google "Tone Policing". In a nutshell, it's when non-BIPOC try to dictate how BIPOC should express their frustrations and experiences in a way that is more "comfortable' for non-BIPOC to absorb. Don't be the Tone Police. If you feel any discomfort, imagine the discomfort of actually enduring these injustices, day after day.

Oh yeah, one last family thing that recently jumped onto my radar as I was finishing this Foreword: my 9 year old son, his name is Teeias. He is named after my late uncle, Loren "Teeias" Thomas, my dad's brother. Loren died during a fishing accident when I was just a toddler. I hardly remember him, but I do remember his face. He was a true activist, present at many "protests". Here he is at Wounded Knee, South Dakota, 1973 (leaning against the back tire). My people have been fighting for what's right, from the beginning. My descendants will know that I stood up for our rights; I peacefully protected; I educated the world; I overcame racial barriers; and I did things few before me did.

I am Jason Eaglespeaker, Blackfoot & Duwamish.

I am a father, I am a brother, I am a son.

I will not be silenced ... we will not be silenced!!!

DEAR GEORGE FLOYD

by Annie Wesley, 80 years old

I embraced you as you lay dying.
Helpless, scared and alone.
I whispered to you.
"Justice will be done.
Peace be with you, George".

2020 years ago, people stood by and
watched Jesus dragged, stripped and
scourged. He died on the cross, buried in
a borrowed grave. He rose from the dead
on the third day. George, you, too will rise
on the last day, in God's glory.

George, you have died for us,
Black, white and many colors in between
God chose you to bear the cross
To shout to the world a powerful message
Justice for all!

Your death gave voice to the world,

Loud and clear, we hear.
"Love, truth and justice.
Justice for all!

'Peace be with you. George.'"

THE THINGS WE FORGIVE

By Dr Dawn Karima

The Things we forgive begin with a
stutter,
Weave into a whisper,
Wrapped in a scream.

We sew medicine into beads and feathers,
And leather, to make them heal in our
dreams.

The weight of the heart is a cruel
transaction,
Measured in virus, wind and blood,
And mud.

Water, a weapon of too much or too little,
Exacting revenge for our toxins in tears.

Years of crying, our relatives fight dying,
Weary of the poisonous things we forgive.

UNTITLED

By Kayla Ironstar

The suits tried to conform us.
They tried to savagely kill us.
Using inhumane objectives
to civilize us.

Brown. Black. Half-breed. Human.
We our alive with the echoes
of voices. Our trills.
Together in song.
The stories of our people
were never to die.

Martin Luther King. Sitting Bull.
Rosa Parks. Tecumseh. Malcolm X.
The history is strong and powerful,
with legacies tracing
to the fight of Tennessee,
Wounded Knee, New York, and Battle of
Batoche.

An unseen power unearthed within our
grassroots community. We will breathe
with our spirits, our voices and our songs.

The healing of our voices and swaying of
dance, we are a peaceful power. We will
stand with our ancestors with spirit and
fire.

Feel the fire and feel the air, the energy is
dancing with change. Change of people,
legislation and paper. I see this: the hunger
strikes, the marches, flash mobs and signs.
No longer will we stand by and witness the
destruction of our People.

You are my brother, you are my sister. Our
People. One Earth.

Where are we to turn when our leadership
defies? Growing in spirit and standing
together, we are waging war for the
people, our future generation.

Gaining momentum of the movement,
we begin to march, drums in hand,
echoes of voices and the presence of
our ancestors. We are together. Hear the
roaring of the people, see the hands
that care.

Feel the energy rising and step forward.
We are the roots for our Mother, we are
change for the people. Gather and pray -
for this is the end and a new beginning.

It is time to re-claim.

HIS HAIR TELLS A STORY

By Kelly Tudor

His hair tells a story.
You see a little brown boy with long hair
and you say it's *"just hair."*

He sees the ships coming to declare
"convert or die."
He sees their dogs ripping The People
apart.
He sees them smash the babies against
rocks.
He sees them building walls to keep us
out.

He sees the words *"merciless Indian
savages"* in the **Declaration of
Independence**.
He sees them going west in the name
of **Manifest Destiny** saying this land is
theirs.
He sees the old newspaper titles that say

"Kill them all, big and small, nits make lice" and *"The only good Indian is a dead Indian."*

He sees fields of massacred People and burned homes.
He sees their scalps being sold for a bounty.
He sees the **Navajo Long Walk** and the **Trail of Tears**.

He sees children kidnapped from their families and sent away to boarding schools.
He sees their hair cut off and lying on the ground.
He sees their clothing and sacred items being burned in front of them.
He sees the children beaten and starved for daring to be Indian.

He sees his great grandmother being sold away from her people less than 100 years ago.

He sees the prisoner of war camps called **reservations**.
He sees pipelines snaking across the land.
He sees **Oak Flat** get sold and mined.
He sees his homelands being destroyed.
He sees the broken treaties.

He sees racist cartoons singing *"what made the red man red."*
He sees racist sports logos and the words that were made to hurt him as team

names.
He see people spit at him and throw trash
at him for holding a sign that says *I am
not a mascot.*
He sees fake headdresses and costumes
while people drunkenly mock who we are.
He sees the costume wigs called *Indian
hair.*

He sees the stoic wooden Indian outside
the tourist shops. It has long hair.
He sees Native boys get their hair cut by
their teachers in front of the class because
"boys have short hair."

He sees his all white baseball team pull
him out of the boy's bathroom and throw
him in the gravel.
He sees them laughing and calling him a
girl.
He sees none of the adults do anything
about it.

He sees the grown men accost his family at
a restaurant to tell them their *"daughter"*
doesn't belong in the men's room.
He sees the grown men get mad and
confused when they walk into the men's
room, too.
He sees the racism directed at him by
children and adults alike.

He sees their words cut into a wound that
is 500 years old.
He sees his ancestors.
He sees those who fought invasion and

colonization.
He sees **Geronimo, Cochise, Victorio**
and **Lozen**.
He sees his people fight the **Apache Wars**
well into the 20th century.
He sees them fight for their people and
ways of life.

He sees their hair grown long like his.
He sees those doing whatever they can
to not only survive, but pass on their
traditions.
He sees resilience.
He sees strength.
He sees resistance.

He sees the **Occupation of Alcatraz**.
He sees **The Longest Walk** and **Trail of
Broken Treaties**.
He sees **Wounded Knee 1973**.
He sees tipis on the National Mall.
He sees the **American Indian Religious
Freedom Act of 1978**.

He sees The People practice their cultures
and beliefs legally for the first time in
hundreds of years.
He sees the **Indian Child Welfare
Act** to protect our children from more
assimilation.
He sees the warriors at **Oka** ... they have
long hair.
He sees the grandmothers and mothers
raising the next generation traditionally.
He sees those grandmothers take down a
Nazi flag and run them out of town.

He sees a boy from his nation fight the
second highest courts for the right to wear
long hair to school in 2006.
He sees the boy win against the school and
wear his hair proudly.

He sees the warriors ride by him at
Standing Rock and say to him "look at
that warrior hair."
He sees those same warriors serving the
Elders breakfast, lunch and dinner before
they get their own plates...so he does the
same.

He sees the responsibility he has to his
people.
He sees thousands of The People march
with him in Washington D.C. to protect
our treaties and rights.
He sees the men at the drum with long
hair.

He sees **Indigenous People's Day** and
Rock Your Mocs week.
He sees **Eugene Brave Rock** and **Adam
Beach** and **Zahn McClarnon** on TV.
They look like him.
He sees books by Native authors that tell
our own stories.
He sees tradition.
He sees culture.
He sees his ancestors.

You look at him and you see *"just hair."*
He sees ALL of that.

TALKING WITH MY SISTERS

By Deirdre Lee

On January 27th, 2017
I went to a memorial
For more than a thousand lost siblings
& I felt myself shatter

Into ten times that many tiny things
Felt my breath catch
& get caught

I am no match
for this loss & grief so profound
For this somehow simultaneously silent
& yet thunderous sound
Of thousands of voices raised, each
singing their sorrow
& their story

Sorry,
but never have I felt this kinda conscious
of the people around me

White folx predominantly
Here in this gallery
At this university
In this municipality

When I traveled out west to the prairies
It was nearly the undoing of me
Surrounded, suddenly
By a continuum of Indigenous identity

NOT that visibility is ANY guarantee of
safety
Paradoxically, the opposite can actually be
true
For me anyway, IDK about you
I don't know if I know more now, or less

I know I can't find the word ... it's not
sadness or stress
Or it's both, but that's like calling the
Rockies a hill
Or the Pacific a puddle, & some people
will
But those people have probably never
walked a path so red
Like life's blood it pushes
my chest drums
& my head

Does its best to just float away
But I stare at my feet on the path & I stay
Asking
in this room full of art how can beauty
hurt this much?
When each stitch & stroke must have been
the source of such mourning,

but perhaps healing too
& my heart beats one question

What do I do
What do I do
What do I do

As I try to commit to memory
Each bead sewn
Each seed sown
Each soul thrown
Out before they were done
In some cases before they had even begun

Tell me,
Which phrase rhymes best with:
I am overcome with the urge to fall down
tear at my clothes
& scream?

Should I just say how badly I want this to
be a bad dream?
That I wanna go off grid & form some
kinda vigilante team?
How can I make jokes when emotions are
this fraught?
How can I still be here,
still breathing,
when so many of us
are not?

Am I still around because I'm meant to
use this loud voice
Get up each day & make the deliberate
choice

Not to shut up or put up or give up or give
in
Til each one of my Indigenous relations
can begin
to know peace truth & wealth
Abundance safety & health

Whatever it takes
Everything is at stake
For all of us still here,
for all those grieved everywhere
I speak these words

Creator, please hear my prayer

THE RCMP

By Marlin Legare

A proclaimed hunger for justice,
A silent thirst to kill.
I have the right;
Just give me a reason or two.
Both of those hands in your pockets will
do.

You've got to be an addict and a thug.
I must assume that you're a murderer, or
at least on drugs.
I smile.
You're too powerless to fight, too poor to
sue.
The public eye scorns, the journalists cry,
"Why does another innocent person have
to die?!"
We huff and we sigh.
Charade lazily,
"Our Thoughts and Prayers are with the
family."

Open tears.
Closed laughter.

This man again? What is he after?!
He'll never learn his lesson,
I'll f*ckin' learn him.
His drunken stumbles have stumbled on
my nerves...
THE LAST F*CKING TIME!

He'll learn his lesson.
I think a long walk home will sober him
up,
Them Indians walk or ride stolen bikes,
When they're not stealing cars,
Or stabbing each other in dykes or in bars
He'll learn his lesson.

The Cold.
The Cold bites with the fury of one
thousand suns
A thousand suns I wish for in the dark, the
complete unknown.
Where am I?
Wet feet trudge towards nothing, towards
a thought and a prayer
I cry.

The wind laughs at my misery and lashes
my skin, my lips and my heart are sealed
I know that this it. I am condemned to die.
Dead feet trudge a dead man,
I am afraid.
Will I ever see my family again? My heart
bleeds.
For I know I will not see them, they will
only see me.

Dead feet trudge a dead man,

I fall.
Violent shaking, dead calmness of night.
Vivid visions of spectacular colours dance.
Ancestors perform on this virgin stage of
snow, ice and wind.
I watch the dance. No strength left to
trudge.
The ice embraces me; I feel warmth for the
last time.

I am afraid.
I don't want to go,
But must be brave,
I accept my doom.

The RCMP
Chose this field as my tomb,
The ice as my grave.

CREATOR!
GOD!
Whoever is there,
Whoever can hear.
Why am I not dead yet?
Why have you forsaken

A Red Man
To turn Blue?
I repent,
I was once lost, but now am found
I was blind, but now I see
If only someone knew I was here
If only shards have ice have not blinded me
If only I wasn't just an inconvenience in
the eyes of the RCMP.
I am free.

"He learnt his lesson",
Say the Children of God.
"He got what he deserved",
Say the Children of God.
"That's what happens when you get
drunk",
Say the Children of God.
"It was all his fault, really",
Say the Children of God.

"His peaceful death was a blessing; he was
saved from being lost. He was a drunk and
a sinner, doomed for the flames of Hell.
Now he's with Jesus, Death saved him from
himself."
Say the Children of God.

Whatever happened to that ol' drunk?
The one that we taught?
How come he is not here to thank us?
That's just like them.
So entitled,
So victimized.

We are here to make you feel safe,
We are here to turn the Red to Pink,
We are here with a secret lust for blood,
We are here to bury language in the mud,
We are here to rape life, destroy peace,
We are here to keep The Problem policed,
We are here dutifully,

We are the RCMP

I AM METIS, I AM WHOLE, I AM ONE

By Tammy Galinec

Never knowing who I should be
I Suffered growing pains
Roots hidden so deep, you cannot see
The blood flowing through my veins

Secrets Kept from light of day
A path I was not shown
Denied my right of way
Shallow lies were grown

A history no one could blame
I believed to protect me
Was a denial born of shame.
For no one else to see

Struggling to know where I belong
I sought the Rest of me

On the wind a whisper of a song
Where grows the tree of my family?

Wading through the lies a family has sown
Lost and alone I could not see
My Shallow roots unknown
Longing to be free

We cannot change the direction
Once our Freedom is gone
In natural selection
Of the path we grow upon

Yet through the cracks a ray of light
No more lies locked in a room
What once was wrong is now made right
Hope begins to bloom

Truth revealed by the light of day
My tiny Roots have grown
This is the only way
The only path I've known

I Never should have been denied
By Shame that was so wrong
Because of those who lied
Even as a Child I did not belong

A lifetime was fought
No longer standing on the sideline
Truth revealed, finally brought
An understanding of what is mine

My whole life a drum beat within my heart
Everything I always believed in
I'm No longer set apart

No longer is my history hidden

I know now with most certainty
As so many search for reparations
I belong with my little stunted tree
My heart soars with the First Nations

The truth no longer will they hide
My branches reach to the sun
Far Past those who have lied
I am Metis, I am whole, I am one.

"My History was denied. For 50 years I had no answers. I once believed it was to protect me. I now know, they wished to avoid shame. My Blue Eyed Mom kept me from Family for a year, so I would not be taken like my Older Brother had been. One day, Mom took me to the Woolworth's Store. I was allowed to pick anything I wanted, despite our poverty. My decision was hard because I wanted both a Drum and a Headdress!

I know now, Women are not supposed to wear Headdresses...but even as a Small child my Ancestry called to me. I was so Proud that day. In that moment, I had no idea I was an embarrassment to my family. People who would not only deny my history, but would many years later tell me they 'never had a problem with it', despite the racism that was very apparent. The hole in my Heart is finally healing."

HONEY BEE HIPS

By Deirdre Lee

Some dude once told me
that my hips could start a war
& I replied
Oh honey that is not what they were made
for

Just like bees weren't created for the
purpose of stinging
Oh honey don't you know anything?
I bet you think water is for selling
& sage is too

I bet you think minimum wage
is good enough for those
you call heroes
But not for you

I bet you don't get
that hard truths could use some gentle
telling

I bet you always gotta have someone
around spelling out the obvious
You think I make a fuss
because I feel disrespected?
Honey, I'm just being protective

I know where my loyalty dwells
It's with the earth & seas it's with the trees
& shells
It's with those willing to or already going
thru hell
To stand together for all our relations
To honour past & present & future
generations
This revolution comes complete with
reverberations

That reveal the power
Of these lips
These hips
Singing
Swinging

Bringing forth art
Like art is life
Like a poem or a song can lift us up out of
strife
Like we can wear our scars like the stripes
on a bumblebee
Proudly
Openly
& Why not?

Technically bumblebees aren't capable of
flight
So how about fck the statistics & systems

that say we're not right?
This fight
Is not over
It is planetary
It is everywhere
Is what the wind tells me

As she pushes past my hair
To reach my ear
This, I need to hear
You need to hear this
We cannot miss
Any more opportunities
To save ourselves our babies

We are seeds
We must revitalize photosynthesize
conceptualize realize
Natural justice
Before the coral & the salmon & the
honeybees are gone
& along with them
All of us

50 SHADES OF BROWN

By Killa Cha'ska

Justice is not justice when it's just us who
suffer
when you need to fit yourself into a box:
White, Black or Other
and you still argue about the existence of
race as if it's not a real thing,
as if you forget all about these boxes you
keep putting us in.

But what happens when that box is made
of wood, it's a coffin.
Or when that box that's checked off is
captioned
"MISSING", "MURDERED",
"FORGOTTEN".

When the amount of melanin in my skin,
determines the life I'm forced to live,
what happens then?

Is it justice when it's just us who need to
justify our reactions?
When you eat from the buffed hands of
the rich
and all we're left with are rations?
When you kill unarmed people do your
fears justify your actions?

Our system is flawed.
"Not guilty,"
"Not guilty,"
"NO repercussions."

I'm so sick of the news these days,
Black boys getting bullets in their bodies
and it's just another day.
Muslims getting bullied because of the
way that they pray
Native children getting put in white
homes and they got no say.

Why is it that when a white guy shoots up
a theatre he gets apprehended?
But when Trayvon walks home with a bag
of Skittles his life gets ended?

And you still have the audacity to say that
"race is not a thing"
Then why am I three times more likely to
go missing?
Five times more likely to have my body
bloodied and found in a ditch?
More likely to become someone's bitch so
they can sell my body to the hungry.

We all bleed the same blood.

But that "flesh" coloured band-aid that's
meant to "conceal as we heal"
is as effective as those temporary
government fixes,
trickier than a turn on a rigged roulette
wheel.

These issues need surgery, not a mere
band-aid fix.
They hit my home harder than a
downpour of bricks
and only when all of our homes start to
crumble at their core
you'll hear our voice, like wild lions we'll
roar.

It's called privilege when you've got the
right complexion for protection.
In this struggle for survival, we're still
fighting the wars of natural selection.
You treated us like rodents.
You tried to exterminate us.

You thought we would disappear.
Well guess what?
We are STILL here.

But we're still dressed in this cloak that
you use to oppress us.
It's heavy, it's dark, and it weighs down as
a means to distress us.
Instead of our dreams
Your invest in our nightmares
And tell us that our worries are not yours.

Racism is that bite that some people can't

seem to swallow.
It's like a tapeworm that eats us raw from
the inside
until it leaves us hollow.
The distrust of the system is rampant.

Why wouldn't it be?
After all of the years we've fought it, it still
hasn't broke me.
Sure I'm cracking, a little banged up and
bruised
all that pain and trauma is the match to my
fuse.

Right now we live in this land of
impunity.
But I want to live in a world that revels in
the idea of solidarity.
I grew from the seeds of a radical story.
We've been rewriting "His-story" and all
of its "glory".

Living through over 500 years of
resistance,
like my father would say, "we're fighting
the longest war in existence".
We can't be a society that only comes
together in the midst of catastrophe.
When we hear those voices shake ...

"No Don't Shoot" and
"I Can't Breathe"

We must continue to assert that we are all
Idle No More
And then like never before we can rise up

from the ashes
from all the times we've been burned.
The heat from those flames will bond us
together like jail bars.
The ones they throw us in where our faces
don't match those of the guards.

We say "united we must stand, because
divided we'll fall"
so let's stand up against injustice once and
for all.
We can't shoulder this burden and
dismantle the system alone
all we have are our guts, our voice, our
hearts and our backbone.

What we need are your blood, sweat and
tears
to soften the blow and to soften the fears.
Don't be afraid to have your back against
the wall.
You can choose to tower over us with the
oppressor
Or stand in the corner with us and believe
in justice for all.

I won't dilute my words
so don't tell me to hush down.
When you're living knee-deep in shit
it isn't something you can tiptoe around.

As an ally to my Black Brothers and
Sisters, with this I will close
I promise to stand in front of whatever
punches are thrown.

BLACK LIVES MATTER
BLACK LIVES MATTER
BLACK LIVES MATTER

Your life matters.
We can't close this book,
But we can write the next chapter.

THUNDERBIRD RISING

By Stephanie Big Eagle

It wasn't legal for Native Americans to practice our religion until 1978. Let that sink in.... 42 years ago. That's in my father's lifetime. We couldn't even burn sage without the risk of imprisonment!

We didn't gain the right to vote until 1965. Also within my father's lifetime at only 55 years ago.

Every one of us you come across today, no matter what our "blood quantum," is a survivor of the largest unacknowledged mass extermination attempt - GENOCIDE - in history, and the cultural genocide continues!

Every reservation is a prisoner of war camp, literally. They each have their own POW number. Our ancestors were herded and held there, by gunpoint. Children were forcibly removed from parents and literally tortured in Christian boarding schools and released back into the world as broken, fragmented, and "assimilated" shells.

Most reservations today are comparable to third world countries. This is by design.

Native Americans are killed by police at a higher rate TODAY than any other ethnic group, and targeted by the justice system to comprise a disproportionately high percentage of the inmate population compared to other races. For example, in Rapid City, SD, the Native civilian population is around 11%, while the Pennington County Jail Native inmate population is about 95%.

If there is any other people who know what it means to be oppressed and targeted by the American system, it is us. This is why we have to support the #blacklivesmatter movement. Our struggles are wrapped up together, and for both of us to make the ultimate change, we have to unite our forces. It is the only way. The government fears us. That is why we are targets. But they underestimated our power, the power of raw survival and resilience.

CULTURAL IDENTITY CONFUSION

By Jocelyn Paul

As a First Nations (FN) woman my past has shaped how I see the world. I was born and raised along the Burrard Inlet, but I am Mi'kmaq, and many of my ancestors hail from the east coast.

Growing up on reserve still (Tseil-Watuuth), I noticed in school, and other activities outside of school, how non-Indigenous students would often refuse to hold hands with Indigenous students, or "be their partner or in their group", and would examine the characteristics of young innocent First Nations youth with disgust.

I also remember some non-Indigenous children making snarky comments, and cruelly cackling at regalia (e.g., headdresses), when represented at various cultural school events.

Overall, I think the most prominent experience I had was in grade 5. My class had this sort of Puberty/Drug & Health Teacher, and she passed out worksheets from a workbook that required critical thinking. One of the questions that the worksheet wanted us to ponder was, what we would do if we were offered cigarettes. The sheet un-settlingly relayed the question, as to how our friend, who lived on the reserve, got cheap cigarettes on reserve, and long story short, was really, really, encouraging "us" to smoke with "them".

Now, this was a worksheet, copied from a textbook. I was young, and had about 6-7 of 35 other Tseil-Watuuth students in my class. Long story short, all of the Indigenous students (as the teacher said we were allowed to work in pairs, if we needed) wrote RACISM all over the worksheet, and we all received a 0/10, despite most of us answering the 9 other questions that were more restrictive or absent of racial undertones - wherein I'd say 8 of the 10 of us were consistently, over the years, A- and above students.

That was the first time, I could just sense and see the pain that colonization and centralization had caused, and that overall: if you were unwilling to fit in and be quiet and stick to the ideas of the higher ups, you would not succeed in life - unless you were embraced colonization and non-Indigenous culture and corresponding attitudes.

I think that - was one of the most eye-opening moments, and absolutely, overwhelmingly terrifying moments, of my life. While I have countless numbers of non-Indigenous mentors that have embraced my Indigeneity, and been overwhelmingly supportive in my success in life, and I have many non-Indigenous friends and I do not blame racism on non-Indigenous peoples of our time - this racism is embedded within our systems.

I blame our colonial tactics, stemming from 1867, when the Indian Act in Canada was indoctrinated. That is what I blame - and that we have let some peoples coming centuries before us - to tell us how we should teach our bright and bushy-tailed youth.

I think it's time for change - and I think that change needs to come as soon as possible. To protect us, the spirit is of our ancestors, and our non-Caucasian allies.

#IndigenousLivesMatter

#BlackLivesMatter

Wela'loiq.

WHAT DOES SHE SEE?

By Chad Haggerty

There were times when I would catch her looking at me. No. Not looking at me, looking through me. I would call her, try without success to get her attention. Wave my hand to break her gaze, if only to tell her that her cigarette was burning her fingers. She couldn't see me. She rarely saw me. It happened so often that I got used to her looking through me, to her not seeing me. I grew used to her staying lost, to cigarettes burning down in her hand.

Cigarettes and stale beer, wrapped like a hand around my throat. Necklace and shirt, torn from my body. Cold evening air taking the breath forced from my lungs. Why did I wear a skirt? I should never have worn a skirt. Stop. please stop...

I grew accustomed to making up stories wherein my mom was as attentive as the mothers my friends had. There were times when she was attentive; she could be fierce and protective, loving and nurturing. We would make eye contact and I would know she was seeing me. She would see me so intensely, her face full of raw, confused emotions, that I wanted her to look through me again. These rare times when she would squeeze me against her and tell me she loved me left me confused and upset.

Those eyes. Stop. His eyes. Stop! Fight. Scream. Do something. Push. Get him away.

Those eyes. Stop. Not his eyes. Stop! Calm. Breathe. Do something. Pull. Hold him close.

When she looked through me, was she remembering the violation? Was she thinking about the innocence she lost, the innocence she birthed?

Is this child innocent? Does he carry a part of the monster that created him?

Was she trying to find peace in her mind, seeking equilibrium? Perhaps trying to find the balance between a life torn apart and a life created? Or maybe she was just trying to wall away the memories to protect herself (and me?) from the hurt that they caused? Was she wondering how to see me without seeing him? How could she show me that she loved me in the face of all the hatred that bubbled up around the memories I carried for her, the horrors I forced her to relive? I got used to blaming myself, to thinking that I had done something wrong.

I learned that it wasn't my fault. Nor was it hers. I was thrust upon her. I wasn't a child begotten of love and affection, of tender memories and remembered romance. I was 19 when I heard the story, the story of when she was 19. The year she gave birth to me, the year she can't forget. In a halting voice, she skipped through the story. She related the bare bones of a story about her bare body. Suddenly I could see what she saw.

She stopped when I couldn't hear any more.

I told her I was ok because she couldn't have heard any less.

THE NOTHING DIRTY LITTLE INDIAN

By Elaine McArthur

"Cops are here!" my sister calls from the living-room.

'Shit' I thought to myself. I slowly get up, my heart is racing and a sense of overwhelming dread envelops me. I really didn't want to talk to them.

They interview me in the kitchen, I tell them everything that happened, again.

"Start from the top" he says to me.

He didn't take off his shoes, and mom had just washed the floor. None of us are allowed to wear shoes in the house. He still had his black hat on, with a shiny black peak and yellow stripe. 'Royal Canadian Mounted Police' on his hat, it's now in my face, and the paleface with blue eyes and freckles is breathing coffee breath up my nose.

"I spoke to the principal and he said he never laid a hand on you." he says with an ugly smirk on his face. "Now, wanna tell me again what happened?"

"I told you." I reply

"Tell me again!" he barks.

I jump and tell myself, 'Don't cry. Don't cry.'

"M-m-my friend, Kathy and I were going to walk to Regina so she can find her brother." I begin, "Then a cop picked us up and took us back to the school. He took us to the principal's office and then went into his office. Mr. Fitch came in and went into the office as well. The cop left and Mr. Fitch told me to come in first. Mr. Parker, the principal told me to sit down on the chair against the wall. He started yelling at me asking where I was going. I said to Regina. Then he grabbed me by the collar of my jacket and twisted it, he pulled me up out of my seat and was yelling in my face, telling me I'd end up a hooker or better yet, dead. Mr. Fitch just stood there glaring at me. Mr. Parker, threw me back into the chair and said, he wished he could beat me. Said that us dirty Indians don't belong in his school."

"You sure you're not lying?" the officer demanded, shoving his pen in my face.

"Hey!" my mom yelled at him, "you don't speak to her like that. Have some respect!"

The RCMP officer said, "I need to determine if she's telling the truth."

He turns back towards me, leans in close and sneers, "Nothing, dirty little Indian is right. Stop the lies." He stood up and wrote something down. "Now what else?"

I stopped, I couldn't speak. I was petrified. I wasn't lying, but he kept getting more and more mad at me.

"Anything else?" he demanded to know.

"I think you're done here for now." mom stood up and walked between us.

My mom, so tiny and so fierce, a twisted dishtowel in her hand, she stood straight, looked up at the officer, and firmly said "YOU CAN LEAVE NOW" - in a voice that leaves no room for argument.

He stared at her and left.

I ran to my room, turned on my music, buried my head in my hands and sobbed until I couldn't find any more tears. Mom came into the room and said, "If you don't want to talk to them again you don't have to. We'll drop the charges." she was brushing my hair back, speaking in a soothing voice.

I nodded and wiped my tears away. After she left, I stared up the posters on my wall and wished I was far away from this. I wished this had never happened to me. It was like a nightmare, mom and dad hadn't even given me shit for walking somewhere without their permission.

Once my parents found out what the principal did, they were furious, and immediately phoned the police to press charges. I cried again, and wished they never called them, they were so mean and ugly to talk to. They scared me.

When the RCMP returned, I saw him in the front yard, getting out of his vehicle. My mom ran outside to meet him. I heard her telling him to leave.

"You scolded her enough to make her drop the charges. You're supposed to help kids, not bully them and scare them. You can get the fuck out of here and never come back. You saved your friend, you piece of shit."

I saw the bastard tip his hat at mom, walk back to his car and then he saw me in the window. He smiled an ugly smile and drove off.

I was 13 years old and chose to return to residential school, rather than go back to a town school.

I AM A METIS WOMAN

By Kali Desautels

I am a Métis woman.

I raised my hand. I looked around. I was alone, timid, and glaring. I raised my hand when prompted by the teacher so she could identify the Indigenous people in the room.

The course was on Indigenous oral history. Our history. I was alone.

The professor identified as English-Canadian. A settler. To teach our histories and our traditions....to us. She who did not even understand, appreciate or know our history was tasked with teaching it at a university.

She taught a classroom of white, and brown, and mixed faces. She asked on the first day whether there were any Indigenous persons in the class. I looked around as I raised my hand and I was alone, and timid, and glaring.

I attended the University of British Columbia for my Bachelor of Arts. I checked the box labelling me as a Métis. I was evaluated and screened and welcomed to class. Evaluated for my grades. Screened for my history. Welcomed for my Indigeneity. Other schools had denied me and then noted the box that labeled me and recanted their denial. The history of me and us greater than my grades and history and knowledge of Canada. I attended and learned and observed. In class he laughed as he spoke of the students like us and denouncing me and my brothers and sisters as space-takers, and invalid and unvalued. We were there because the Canadian government felt guilty for the harm, he told us. She laughed when he looked at her because she believed it, too. I was told by my peers that I had a space at the school merely because of the box that I had checked. My years of study and learning and trying were reduced to simply a box.

I signed up for a course on Indigenous oral history led by a professor who did not understand and appreciate and know our history. She was an Anglo-Canadian who taught English literature and travelled the world and felt entitled to teach what she saw but did not know.

Throughout the course, this woman, this professor, she had us sit on our desks, so we could form a settler's vision of a medicine wheel, a talking circle. She instructed us to "confront" First Nations people. She directed us to walk into "reservations" or visit Vancouver's Downtown Eastside, where we were sure to meet some of "them".

Whup, Whup, Whup. As she spoke, I could almost hear the flock of Thomas King's Indians flying into the windows.

"A family from Buffalo came through last week and didn't even see an Ojibwa."

Just like the dawn cleaners of King's A Short History of Indians in Canada, the professor instructed us with no regard for the white gaze or her gaze or their gaze. She saw us, our Indigenous personhood, our uniqueness, our intractable selves as specimens. She gave us three questions and instructed us to approach First Nations, and Métis, and the people existing on the margins and demand answers.

I took my questions. She brought her spotlight to my seat in her talking circle. She demanded that I explain myself, explain my Indigeneity to the class, and explain how this is how they should learn. This is how they would become more aware. This is how they would check their privilege. But in those days, we did not check our privilege, I did not demand that white people do more than feel comfortable and I did not express rage at being the significant Other.

She told us to look for a feather on the road, because that feather was a gift to us. She told us that feathers are only given to those who see them. But we see them. We see them on the ground and the road and the grass and the birds.

We see them swept aside on the Downtown Eastside and the Highway of Tears.

I took my feather and my three questions and looked in the mirror. I asked myself "When did you first encounter a white face?" The face in the mirror is white. Because it is white, and it is Métis and it is mine. It was the first.

I asked myself "what is it like to be an Indigenous person?"

I tilted my head and questioned my reflection and wondered when I knew that I was, and I wasn't. In those days, Métis was not even recognized. This was before. But then and now I am Métis.

I asked myself "what would you like the rest of Canada to know about you?"

I pursed my lips and thought that I wanted the rest of Canada to know that I and us and we are not on display. I thought that I wanted the totem poles and artefacts to go home. I thought that I wanted the rest of Canada and my professor and my classmates to know that I am here and valid and valued.

I wrote a paper answering the questions and I answered them for myself. I did not need to be told where to find an Indigenous person, because she is with me everywhere. She is with me when my classmates laughed about my ancestors and the jugs of moonshine and how they saw me. Like a cartoon from a 1950s newspaper. Sprawled and brown and mean. She is with me when my professor professed her ignorance and pointed to me instead of educating me. She is with me when I felt shame and red cheeks and anxiety because I was the Other. She is with me when I entered the ceremonial door at my Aboriginal graduation and sat on the stage with my sisters and commenced my life out of the place of learning.

The learning where I learned that I was not one of them. The learning that thought that this woman, this professor, this settler had the knowledge necessary to teach our history, while knowing nothing of our history. Except for circles, and feathers, and margins.

AN EASY TARGET

By Maria Guzman

Part I

In the early 1970s, in a small town where nothing besides children climbing the neighbor's trees and stealing its fruits, ever happened, an event occurred which might have surprised even the most skeptical members of society, if they had ever known. A beautiful young woman, 24 years of old, with a very bright and promising future, decided to leave everything behind and venture "off the grid" becoming a hermit.

The decision to separate herself from society, may appear premature to those who did not understand the cause nor the circumstances that brought about such a drastic reaction, but not to her. She acted according to what had worked for her under similar circumstances and thought it best to hide away her remaining years to avoid history from repeating itself.

It being such a small town where everyone knew everybody's business, the members of the families of the participants involved, wondered about the motives she may have had, but no one took the time to investigate and moved on.

She came from an impoverished family but was raised with high moral values. Her bright future included studying at the university, though she did not know what her major would be.

She locked herself away from all mundane activities, going out only to do the essential tasks for staying alive and continued to go to college but, for self-protection, she kept her distance from others.

She had recently moved to town from a major city where she had been sexually assaulted as a teenage girl. An incident she kept to herself, thinking she could get past it and never got the help she did not know she needed. The small town seemed like the perfect setting to start a new life.

She had very humble and troubling beginnings. Her father, raised to believe women were inferior to men, abandoned her mother with three children, two girls and a boy, ages ranging from 6 months to five years. He left with the promise that he would send for his wife and children as soon as he got a job in the city.

At such a young age, the two girls had to help their mother with the chores, going to the public fountain, barely dressed, to gather water, subjecting themselves to men's and boy's lusting eyes and comments. They would wash the clothes and clean the small residence before their mother arrived from working at the sugar cane plantation.

A year after her father left, and realizing her husband would not keep his promise, her mother had no choice but to give up her two girls. They went to live with her father's sister, starting a journey of moving from one relative to another. Many years would pass before they saw their mother again.

For the first couple of years, her mother would visit her girls every month, but it soon became clear to her that her husband's sister did not care very much for her and her visits. They were cruel and inhospitable to her.

For years, the girls spent most of their time alone with nature, roaming around, climbing trees, bathing in the streams, and eating seasonal fruits which they gathered by climbing the trees. Their aunt, a daughter and a son were never home. The elder worked at a manufacturing factory and her son and daughter went to school.

Being left alone did not bother the girls for they loved the wilderness and it did not scare them at all. They lived a carefree life and like gazelles they could disappear for hours in the woods where they always found something interesting to do.

Six years after coming to live with their aunt, and under false pretense, their aunt told the mother the girls were going to visit their father in the city for the summer. She would not see her daughters nor hear from them again until they were adults.

Their life in the city was filled with boredom and disappointments. They moved around a lot. They went from one family member's household to another, until the eldest graduated and decided she would become independent.

Their father never really assumed responsibility for his girls. He drank and carried on his life as if he were still a bachelor until he was forced to take a job as a building superintendent and take the girls with him.

He took an older woman as his concubine wife thinking he did not have to support her for she was past Social Security age. He needed someone to take on the responsibility for the girls.

The wife watched soap operas all day and the girls had to do all the chores around the house. When the father got home there was always a confrontation: the evening meal not being on time or the clothes not washed or ironed, and the blame always fell on the girls. The girls barely had time to do their school homework for the chores kept them up till bedtime. They learned to do their schoolwork under the covers of the bed sheets with a flashlight. They did not want their father to find out and scold them for not going to sleep when told to do so. The eldest was already in Junior High School when they came to live with their father and remained with him until she was close to graduating from High School.

She was nearing her last year when the first event that would mark her for the rest of her life, occurred.

She was going steady with a young man much older than her. His name was Angel and the name fit him perfectly. He was the only son in a family where the mother was raising two girls and her son, on her own. Angel had recently been released from the military service where he had been drafted to serve during the Vietnam Conflict. He was the man of the house, caring for his mother and sisters. Angel and she met when they were introduced by his younger sister when she came with her to the house. Angel, being raised with women, treated his girlfriend with love, kindness, and respect.

He could not visit her due to her father's abusive nature. For them to share some time together, he would pick them up from school and bring them to the house for a couple of hours.

Angel's sister had a boyfriend who would also come to the house and on numerous occasions would coincide with her visits to her boyfriend. This young man also lived in the building behind where she lived and spent time peeking out his window, watching her every move from afar. Premeditating!

One day, Angel was not able to pick her up and his sister had not been able to go to school. His sister's boyfriend did. He came to her and told her he had been sent to pick her up and bring her to the house. She had no reason to doubt him, she went with him. But he had his premeditated plans. As they walked from school, he stopped at a candy store and bought them both some sodas.

All she remembers was waking up in an obscured building hallway. She was drowsy and felt like she had been beaten and struck by lightning. She got up and somehow managed to get home. She could not stop crying though she had no idea what had happened to her. She had been drugged and raped! She was never the same!

She stopped going to her boyfriend's home and finally called him on the phone to tell him she did not want to go out with him anymore.

Angel asked her:

——Why are you crying if you do not want to be with me anymore? She was incapable of telling him what she knew in her heart was true. There was nothing she could offer him; it had been taken away so drastically and inhumanely. That was the end of a beautiful relationship!

She carried on with her life, but a rebellious nature had taken the place of pure innocence. She graduated but barely making the grades and enlisted in the military service to get away from her past. She spent the next three years fighting someone else's war, discrimination, and her inner battles.

Part II

Many years had passed before she came back to her mother's house. She started her graduate studies with hope and optimism. She was intelligent but still naïve to evil intentions. She had none!

Her mother had remarried a gentleman who had been a schoolteacher for years and had retired. It was him who saw the girl's promising abilities and skills. He vouched for her, enrolling her in a Board of Education Teaching Program to become a schoolteacher.

She immediately began teaching and continued her studies to obtain her bachelor's degree. She taught from an early age of twenty and one. After a couple of years, she decided she had no vocation for teaching and changed her major to liberal arts. Although she was good at teaching, she felt that was not what she wanted to do for the rest of her life. She loved reading and writing poetry but that would not pay the bills, so she had to teach to support herself. It would not be till her retirement years when she would devote herself to her passion and vocation.

The small town where she was born, and the one she would return to, was divided by classes: the upper class whose members were neither rich nor poor. They were those families whose names could be identified as part of living in this town for decades, considered the town's founding families. Doctors, lawyers, and politicians were among them. The middle class were the working professionals, although they had meager salaries. It included schoolteachers, police officers and lower government officials. The poor class included the sugar cane plantation workers, maintenance, cleaning services, manufacturing workers and the unemployed.

Her mother was a school lunchroom attendant and therefore she was part of the lower class. Her husband had once belonged to the upper class due to his name and profession, but he had become an alcoholic in his later years and spent most of his retirement pay on whisky. Although respected and feared for knowing everyone's sins, he had fallen from the grace of the upper class. He got his wife part time odd jobs as a cook for festivities of the elite, where they would pay her by giving her all the leftover food and 'hors d'oeuvres' to take home to her children.

The young lady did not feel comfortable in the two upper classes, though she was a schoolteacher. She would rather be among the college students she had met. They did not follow any specific set of rules and like most college students, they lived the moment, going to school during the week and partying on weekends. They apparently accepted her in their inner circle, and she accepted them. They spent their weekends in merriment, celebrating one festivity after another: spring breaks, Christmas, birthday celebrations, summer vacations, holidays, and weekends.

If she had stopped to consider, she would have realized she did not belong with them, for they were part of the two upper classes and acted like spoiled brats. She went along with whatever they had going, barely taking the time to study them intimately. What she did not know was that they were morally inferior. The men were male chauvinists by education. Same as her father, they had been taught that women were inferior, meant to do house chores such as cleaning, cooking and taking care of their husbands. They patronized, denigrated them and treated them with less than equal benefits, even if they helped provide for the family.

Part III

She had a cheerful nature and youthful manner which went along with the young adult rebelliousness of the time.

Her birthday was coming up, and she decided to celebrate it. Most of the group members were invited not necessarily by the birthday girl, whom didn't really know most of the visitors in attendance, but word of mouth invitation ran across town like water runs through a risen river and there was a full house.

What happened that night was like a verse from an Edgar Allan Poe poem: brutal and bizarre. Even more like a scene from the Alfred Hitchcock's Presents series. The town's general population would have been appalled, sickened, and horrified and the members of the upper classes would have never imagined nor believed what caused their children to behave in such a hideous, wicked, evil manner.

A young man approached the birthday girl and asked to dance with her. He put a pill in her hand and told her it would do no harm but make her birthday a much happier one. Why she believed it is beyond comprehension.

When she awoke the following morning, she did not remember getting home. Her memory was a blank piece of paper for several months and even years.

Many years later she remembers, or maybe the nightmares that have plagued her for so many years have brought back memories from that tragic night. She sees herself waking up the first time in a strange bed in a dark room of an even darker house, trying to get the naked man on top of her, off of her nude body; at least fifteen other men surrounding her, and a voice that screamed from somewhere in the dark:

——Enough! Leave her alone already!

The second time she woke up she was being forced to walk around for some time and then given a cold shower.

Like a recording, the voice and those words have stayed with her though the faces faded immediately and completely.

It took her many years in isolation to realize why she had been subjected to these heinous crimes. She was a woman, from the lower class, a mixed race of White, Black and Taino Indian: An easy target.

Used and abused throughout her life, she decided it was time to separate herself from the type of society that abuses its own.

LIVING IN TWO WORLDS

By Rudy Kelly

Living in two worlds but never forgetting the "others".

With the horrific killing of George Floyd by a policeman in Minneapolis and protests in the U.S. and around the world, the issue of racism, particularly White on Black and other minorities is dominating the headlines. I haven't talked much about my experiences with racism, even in my columns during my days as a reporter. I figure that now is a good time as any.

Being an Aboriginal in Canada, racism is something that I think about almost every day. It may come to me as a memory of an experience I had, or I might see or hear of someone I know experiencing it. Sometimes, it will come to mind just because of the repercussions of past atrocities, the trickle-down effects of residential schools that have rooted themselves in me.

My personal experience with racism has been varied. Early in life, I experienced the poison variety. Being poor, with rummage sale clothes, and having brown skin and long hair made me somewhat of a poster boy for the term "dirty Indian." For the longest time, I didn't think there was any other kind. It didn't help that I was the darkest in the family, which made me scrub a little harder sometimes.

I dreaded lice checks in school because it was always us dirty Indians that had them and some teachers took pleasure in announcing who needed to pick up a prescription for lice treatment in front of the whole class. I remember being in line at school and overhearing one of the white girls whisper to a friend to stay clear of me because "Rudy always has lice."

I was picked on as a kid, but it wasn't as severe for me as it was for others because I had the implied protection of tough, older brothers. And, having been toughened up by those brothers, I handled myself well enough that most bullies in my age and weight class didn't bother me. There were times, though, when I was harassed by pairs or groups of white guys a few years older than me. Not being one to just take shit, I often talked back to them and that, occasionally, resulted in a shot to the head.

A lot of how someone experiences racism has to do with the pecking order. Certain things allowed me to gain a foothold in the white world. To start, I did well in school. I recall my first year in junior high, when a teacher would announce who had the top test or assignment results, I was always in the mix. When I got the top mark, all the non-Aboriginal brainiacs that had come from different elementary schools, couldn't hide their surprise. I felt like Taylor when he first spoke in Planet of the Apes.

Before too long, as I became more outgoing and gained more white friends, they started to think of me as one of them – but that didn't mean they weren't racist. For some of them, I was just one of the good ones. I recall one night when I was in a car with three white friends and we were wondering what to do. One of them said, "let's go downtown and beat up some Indians." There was an awkward moment, and then the guy said, "not talking about you, man. You're not like the others." I suppose that moment was my first as an "apple."

As I continued on through high school I gained more white friends and some of my Aboriginal friends faded away, largely due to them dropping out of school. The trend continued with my going to college for journalism, which was so rare that I was the first Aboriginal person to graduate from the Mount Royal program.

As I became more of a "professional," I faced less racism. I am always wary of it, though, because I know it is never too far below the surface. Several years ago, I was at a conference down south. After having dinner at a local pub, I was walking along when I heard some guys in a truck going by yell, "get off the street, Indian!"

A second later, a beer bottle whizzed by my face and shattered against the wall of the building beside me. They laughed as they sped away. I got off the street alright, and went straight back to my hotel.

I usually feel some unease whenever I travel on my own and I'm always a little nervous walking into an establishment where, as Eddie Murphy's character said in the movie, 48 Hours, when he walked into a country bar, "there aren't a lot of the brothers here."

When I'm home, in Rupert, I feel very safe. That's partly because Rupert has a large Aboriginal population and, for the most part, there is respect for Aboriginal people and culture, and acknowledgement of the wrongs that have been committed against Aboriginal people and the reconciliation that is needed. Being well known locally and fairly well-liked also makes home feel safe.

Another reason that I am relatively safe from racism in Rupert is the same one given by that guy in that car those many years ago: you're not like the others.

The others. I see them all the time. They're on the streets. They're struggling to survive. They're being sneered at and looked down on. No one knows their stories or why they are there. Some people don't care and would like to see them swept under a giant rug.

I may not be in the place "those people" are but I was there. And, sometimes, I am there, whenever I visit family members or friends who live in poverty or battle addictions, or who struggle to cope with the trauma and hardships that resulted from residential schools and systemic racism. To me, they are not the others; they are a part of me, and I'll always have one foot in that world.

For those who have never seen that world, I mean really seen it, you should visit it some time. Go to where they are and pull up a chair. Listen. Stop being a stranger to them. That's the only way that racism withers and dies in anyone; when they take a moment, to meet and, more importantly, understand and know the others.

WHAT'S THE WORST INJUSTICE YOU'VE EXPERIENCED?

Question 1

Nettie Caldera

Cop stopped me and assumed I stole and was driving a stolen car and it was my own car.

Jasmine St Amand

My mom was a 60s scoop. Adopted by a white family with an extremely abusive mother. They took her not even a day after her mother passed in a car accident, my mom was two years old. Ripped them from their siblings, while they screamed and cried. She was adopted after only being at that place for one month.

I've also had run-ins with Thunder Bay police too. I was raised there. I had cops running up to me with their flashlights and everything in my face. Accused myself and 3 other Indigenous kids of being drunk and drinking (we were coming back from the movies and being silly, no alcohol) I got called *feisty* because I was pissed off they were accusing us of this. They even made me open my purse and asked *what's that*. It was an energy drink in my purse. I wholeheartedly believe that if I was alone they would have taken me in. But there were four of us, so I think they only left us alone because of that. They didn't want any witnesses.

Helen Hillman

Getting hired for a job, but when the manager saw me, he said they have their quota of minority workers. They told me they didn't need a new waitress after all.

Candace Macaulay

Got arrested and spent 3 months in custody with no charges because I fought back against a white guy who was trying to assault me. I gave him stitches and he made me black and blue broke my nose, left me with bald spots from him pulling my hair out. They didn't take a mug shot till I got to the women's facility. Which they kept transporting me between three facilities so no one had a chance to make inquiries as to why I was even in custody and the condition I was in.

Zoey White

A cop was called to a scene. Threatens to shoot my grandma and me for "obstructing justice".

The scene: My uncle is drunk and saying he wants to die, so my grandma and I walk over to his house. He says, someone already called the cops, so he can attack them and be shot up.

A Cop arrives, and my grandma begs her son to go back inside the house. He does. That is seen by the officer as obstruction of justice, and he began saying he was going to take us all to jail, all while pointing his gun at all of us. When the second officer arrived, my grandma was so scared she took my hand and ran home. My grandma had surgery on her hip and was told to never run again until that night. I felt terrible when she broke down crying at the house.

Crystie Cloud

My public defender tried to talk me into accepting a deal that the DA had no evidence on!

Aaliyah Calliou

I got stopped on my way walking to school, 'cause I "looked like someone they were looking for", but showed me a picture and looked nothing like me.

Jay Helstrom

I was sent to prison under a wrong name.

Jordan Wabooze

Getting beaten by TBPD officers and taken to the "Farm" and thrown in the hole for couple weeks to heal up, no charges whatsoever. Called my lawyer and he got me out the same day. Judge apologized to me saying "that shouldn't have happened to you, mister". He ordered my release.

Julie Yates

I got beat up by a woman on meth, who broke into my boyfriends' house while I was pregnant. She got a few others besides me, but trashed sh*t. Knocked me around, pulled my hair, scratched at me, and pulled me to the ground, kicking at me.

Her meth pipe fell out of her pocket and was given to police. We made statements, we went to the hospital, we had proof of an injury to my boyfriend's mom. Tell me why that woman got no time in jail, no probation, just a slap on the wrist? And when we tried to get in touch with them, they ignored us. Didn't tell us about the court hearings. Until the last one, where she didn't even show up. And she still got off with time served. And now, she's still on meth, and my boyfriend's mom still has neck issues from getting punched in the head a few times.

Vandee Crane

I was trafficked, and tortured as a child, by a white law enforcement officer, who was supposed to be a family friend

Stacey Huempfner

I almost got ran over by a racist. She knew I was Native because my grandmother lived above her in a duplex. I fell and my aunt, who was younger than me, pulled me out of the way as the lady ran my bike over.

Dorothy Jacobs

Our home was burned to the ground by KKK, while we were all gone to the hospital for my dad's heart attack.

Cheney Yellowquill

I was handcuffed by police and beaten in custody for not talking, cuffed and taken to the river docks and they tried to throw me in.

Elizabeth Boivin

Having our house shot up by FBI, Fed Marshals, county and tribal cops. Swat and every law enforcement officer that could hold a gun. Shot up a house with little kids in it. The next day no one was allowed in the house, 'cause it was shot up so bad. No one knew how it was still standing. I was 7.

Kelly Shaw

Walking into a subway that a group just rushed, after attacking someone down the road. The cops grabbed me, forced me to put my phone and work bag down, then ziptied me, and threw me into a wall. I didn't know what happened, they didn't answer me when I asked what happened. What did I do? I cried, while people watched in disgust. Then the couple came, and the boyfriend points to me and says Ya her!! I'm like what I've never seen you what happened. The girlfriend said NO not her she was never there. Finally the cops listened and let me go, after what felt like forever. I was racially profiled grabbed and held, all while trying to go home.

Ellison R.

Getting raped by an on-duty cop, and I get sent to jail for protecting our water. When I filed a report, a different cop came to my cell and ripped up the report in front of me.

Jordan Henderson

As a 15 year old I got tased and beat by three officers. They let me go after they couldn't take me to the drunk tank, or charge me with anything.

Ryan Three Fingers

An Edmonton city cop was dragging me out the doors by my hoodie, I couldn't see, and then BAM, he pushed me up against a metal gate…he nearly broke my back asking me if I wanted to get my ass kicked, but my family and friends got to see what he did and they spoke up. That's when he realized everyone from our multi-cultured community was watching him.

Albert Linfitt

Physical, racial and emotional abuse from teachers and white students, from kindergarten through to junior high. Teachers standing by and doing nothing, sometimes just watching us fight it out. I'm almost 66 years old now, and remember vividly what happened at age 5. This is what it does to a person. The healing journey becomes life itself.

Rae Wright

Being abducted at 14, escaping, and the police who picked me up wouldn't even take a statement.

Denee Reansbury

My sister and her 4 friends were tased, for streaking down Main Street. You could clearly see they had no weapons, but that didn't matter to RCMP.

I had my brand new car keyed at school, because all Indians do is 'get free money'. I confronted the guy, who bragged he did it and spit on me. My school did nothing. I actually got the car as a grad gift from my grandpa (white), for passing with honors.

A white student pushed me into the lockers and said we were going to fight after school. I show up and she has 20 of her friends. I showed up with me and my boyfriend. I called her a wimp and she said she was afraid I'd jump her with all my cousins. I have 3 cousins and we always fought fair, but because I'm Indian, I'm a cheater?

Hawk Olebar

Went to prison for 10 years, for a crime I didn't commit.

Jeanette Constant

My son in law just got murdered on Mother's Day 2020, and the judge approved of this filthy animal's bail - the one that killed him, he's walking. The system is messed.

Derrick LC

Was beaten by 6 Calgary police officers when I was 16, and tiny. When cuffed and on the ground face down, they started to kick me between the legs with their steel toes.

Star Cardinal

I tried to stop some cops (1 Caucasian, the other was Persian) beating up a woman on a main street in my town. I had just seen her around the corner being assessed by paramedics and she walked away with a little white blanket on her shoulders. Before I got around the block (to check on her and offer a ride), 2 police were literally wiping the street with her, dragging her back and forth on her front, her shirt was pulled way up and her stomach was bleeding. I ran to them and asked them to stop, I explained that she just came from the ambulance and might not be well. They shouted at me to stay back, one pushed me back on my shoulders and shouted if I interfere again, I will get arrested too. I was shaking, but I stood there and watched and said, "I see you guys, big strong men, you don't have to do this." They didn't like me watching and tried to follow me to a vehicle, I ducked into a bar! Then I complained to the staff sergeant, who said if I want to pursue the complaint I will have to confront the officers in person. I said no thanks.

Cyrus Bourassa

Got jumped outside the bar, crawled to the hospital ... then they threw me in the drunk tank instead.

Tamara Edgars

I watched my Indigenous neighbor across the hall get beat by a group of police - 2 male, 1 female. They all had stickers over their badge numbers and the females badge had a sticker over her badge that said "Bitch." My neighbor was screaming for help, saying they were choking her. When I peeked out, they were all standing around laughing, getting a kick out of what they were doing to her. When I showed my face, they all straightened out and stopped. Then, one of the male cops dragged my neighbor all the way down the hall by her hair. The next day I picked up a ball of her hair.

Cedar Kovak

Getting arrested for being intoxicated, and when I said something 'bout my rights, I got taken into a sand pit and was beaten while cuffed. I was 16 at the time.

Tamara Edgars

I got arrested in Nanaimo, BC as a teenager, I don't know why I was singled out from my friends (we were drinking). I have anger like my mom, so when they arrested me I fought back. The cops had me on the ground face down, I managed to turn around and kick the cop in the face, it was the cops 1st day on the job, probably just training the freaking guy. It took 3 cops to stop me and get me into the cop car. I had to write an apology letter to him in court and the cops took photos of my hands saying I'm considered a deadly weapon.

Victorius Capot

Being choked while I was in handcuffs in the back of a police car.

Marie MacDonald

As my father lay dying in a hospital bed at UofA hospital in Edmonton, with many of my large family around, one nurse was particularly rude and unkind. Kept referring to us as "you people" in a demeaning tone, and was so annoyed we were there. Refused to answer questions. Huffed and puffed at every little thing. My dad was dying for goodness sakes! Where was her compassion and care? I'm a white coated First Nations gal, so I rarely experience this kind of treatment if I am alone. But when I'm with my obviously Native family, oh ya, it's blatant. And so very wrong.

Char Anna Rowland

Being taken away from my parents. I was stolen at six weeks old, raised by white people. I'm a 60s scoop child, never got to meet my mom, she died at 26 years old because she wanted us kids back. When I met my dad, he said he didn't know what happened and could not find us when he came back from work. He said my mom would never had let us go, ever, they made up lies to take us away the government.

Lee Gerry

I was beaten by six cops, well, we tussled, they hit me with a baton, it took all of them, I was sober, I got a lawyer, they said they lost the tape and also the DA was sitting shotgun and signed that she witnessed the cops.

Jordan Robles

Getting dragged across my house in submission holds by my white correctional officer step dad, and my mother gaslighting me for 20+ years that shes a good person, only to be barred from my sister's graduation party because "there's gonna be a lot of cops there."

Miki McKitrick

Never being looked at in the face by doctors and nurses, while I spent five days in labor. When they saw my (step) dad...I became human, because he's white. Suddenly, I was rushed into emergency C-Section delivery. My doctor actually looked at me in the eyes, and I said, "Wow, this is what it's like when ur deemed to be human." He apologized. Was nice to be white for a bit lol. The change in level of care was so terribly obvious.

Bobbie Howard

Police taking me to sleep it off, instead of a hospital, when I told him I was raped. And nothing being done about it.

Brody Merrick

Got 300 stolen from me by Brandon police service.

Geo Shaughnessy

Cops throwing 5 Natives in jail, based on a witness that lied. Upon finding out, they tried getting us 5 to pay for damages, to get the charges dropped.

Amy-Leigh Marie

I called the police for help and asked for a ride home, because I was in an unsafe situation. During my ride home, the white police officer continued to antagonize me and threatened to drop me off on the side of the highway, with no shoes on. I told him I felt unsafe. I told him I'm a RN, thinking that would make it better, but it didn't. He continued to threaten me, as I rightfully continued to say my rights and how I feel for my safety. It was traumatic, and I no longer have trust in them for any kind of help.

Marie Martinez

When I was in the 3rd grade, I went to a school official on the rez & tried to get help. I was being molested by more than one family member. I got sent to a girls' group home, while things were being handled - only to be told I was being picked up and sent home days later. Yes, back to the same home. I was told I lied, and was making up stories for attention.

Roy Eagle

They coached a witness against me to get a conviction.

Brent Spears

Denied my own high school education, and hidden in my own home for being gay. I worked 5-6 days a week to pay for my testing to enter HINU, left, and was disowned for not hiding myself from public. I now have a beautiful family.

Rena Fabel

Being molested by our medicine man.

Leah Seneca

Being accused of stealing, the store owner swore up and down I stole something. He ordered me to dump the contents of my purse, so, knowing I didn't take anything, I dumped everything out and proved him wrong. He walked away without apologizing. I was 15 years old when that happened.

Tiffany Sanderson

I got the sh*t beaten out of my by 2 cops, who made me sound like I was the criminal - when I was just trying to get home!

Elle McArthur

The principal in my high school choked me once and the police believed him over me. The RCMP officer even called me a "nothing dirty little Indian", and to stop the lies.

Evelyn G.

At age 15 I was a witness to police brutality. I was called to testify at a police hearing inquest. Despite police cover-ups and lies, the inquest resulted in the dismantling of a tactical squad, and a firing of a police chief. I thought my fight was over. But on my 17th birthday I was at an event with my best friend. We happened to meet two guys that were training to become police officers. We got to talking, and when one of the guys realized who I was, he said something like. "Just wait until I become an officer - you better watch your back, 'cause you're going to get yours." I was traumatized and beyond shocked. My witness to a police beating of an innocent 17 year old was proven in law to be true, yet someone - who was not even an officer yet - was out to get me because of what I witnessed.

This all happened 43 years ago, yet my fingers are shaking so bad right now that I can barely type. Needless to say I have had an underlying fear of police ever since. I know there are many good officers out there - but I ask them not to turn the other way when they see a fellow officer misuse their power. Police Brutality scars you for life.

Amelia Sedley

I called the police because I had been assaulted. And the police threatened to arrest ME for trespassing on my own property. I then understood that the police are NOT on my side.

Deb Mohr

A cop named "Hutch" pulled me over because my registration had expired. To make things worse, I had forgotten my wallet so I didn't have my license. I opened my purse to show him that I didn't have my wallet, apologizing profusely. He wrote me a ticket for no license and registration, took a screwdriver to remove my license plate and said, "you are not driving this car." He then got in his car to drive away. We were in an industrial area, not a residential area. There was no one around. It was the end of the day and all the offices were dark. It was cold out and I just had on a light jacket and a skirt. That was before the days of cell phones. I had no money and no way to call someone to drive me home. I told him I was a single mom with four kids at home, one of them a diabetic foster daughter who would need to eat right away. I asked if he could give me a ride home. He ignored me and climbed into his car. I said, "Aren't police supposed to PROTECT? You have now placed me in a very vulnerable position. Look around—it's dark. I'm cold. I'm alone. I already told you I have no money, so I can't call for help…" That as**hole drove away and left me there.

Melanie Sutcliffe

I use to work as a community mental health worker. A client of mine had been beaten by police and they dropped him off with gaping wounds on his head, still heavily bleeding, like he was garbage out front the house.

They were not expecting me to be there looking for him. They did not expect someone to care about him.

This night has been playing over and over in my head lately. For obvious reasons I'm sure. Another that I had not thought about was how privileged I was in the moments that came next.

I hollered and I screamed at that cop. I demanded answers. I demanded medical attention for my client. I took the officers badge number and explained if they left without providing care I would rain down all sorts of fire and hell upon them... never not once did I fear for my safety in that moment. I did not fear being arrested. I did not fear being beaten. I did not fear being killed.

Those thoughts never even entered my mind.

I was covered in blood that night, none of it was my own.

That is the reach of privilege.

Dawn McCormick

I have been fortunate in my life. I have never experienced that type of injustice. However, I have experienced rape, and, when reporting it, found that my words went unheard by the authorities. Mostly men who literally protected the offender because they were friends with him. I wasn't the only victim, but it took a long time to get a police officer to give credence to all the complaints about this man. A sort of MeToo moment, long before that movement.

M.C. Schmidt

The injustices I have experienced as a woman and teenager I will not speak about here, but they have not been by police. What I will say is I'm so done with inequality...I want equality for the Black community, I want it for women, I want it for Indigenous people, and every other race or "difference" someone that has been made to feel like they are less than, by someone or group of people who thinks they are better than. These kinds of changes, and the work it takes to do so, have taken way too long to get finished. So I work every day, to raise my son right and good, I work hard to be of service, to learn and keep an open mind, to listen, to speak with a sensitive heart, to be an advocate and activist behind the scenes away from cameras and spotlight...to be a peacemaker in the best way I know how. I have no interest in my own comforts, if it comes at the price of another's. So much work left to do!

WHEN DID YOU FIRST EXPERIENCE RACISM?

Question 2

Jody Mattena

I was tied to a tree when I was eight years old, so the white neighbors could play "Cowboys and Indians" with a real "Indian". I don't know how long I was left there when they were done, a few hours maybe. It's never left my mind.

Sarah Jones

While I was in middle school, kids would make me open my mouth to see my teeth. They would claim that I was lying about being Alaskan Native, because my teeth were "too perfect". Also, my mom and I get plenty of looks in public when we are together. People in Oklahoma have no freaking clue what an Inuit is, so they would think that we were just super "white Asians"...

Fent Zaak

Getting jabbed continually in the head, with a sharp lead pencil, by my grade 4 Korean teacher. She'd say, "you understand you filthy thing?" I failed grade 4 because of her. You see, it's not just white folks that are prejudice in this World.

Flett Nepinak

In grade 6, my school didn't do anything about the blatant racism there. The kids there would stuff me in trash cans and call me a dirty Indian. My teachers ignored me and told me to get over it. The other kids would follow me home and throw things at me, or tear my clothes. I ended up cutting off all my hair and tried to commit suicide. I ended up moving away, but the fact that the students and teachers got away with it scares me for when my kids go to school.

DeeAnna Holland

I didn't even know it was racism that every time I went shopping with my brown Mom, we would be followed by store employees.

JJ Elliot

From 1st to 5th grade I had a girl compare her hand color to mine every day and call me "white girl", and tell me I am not Indian until finally, the 5th-grade teacher put a stop to it. I will always wonder but will never ask her why, I just think she and her family had a lot of issues, and she selected me to take them out on. I just let others be who they are because of her so I learned a lot from her.

Amanda Figueroa

I was so little that I used to wave and say hello to everyone I saw. Once I said hello to this light skinned older lady, she kept turning her cheek and avoiding me.

I asked my mom, "is she sick, why isn't she looking or talking to me??? She didn't say hello like everyone else did."

I remember being so puzzled, my mom grabbed my hands and nodded and said "she won't ever talk to you or me, she doesn't like us. I kept insisting..why, mom... why????? And my mom snapped and said: ITS BECAUSE OF OUR SKIN!!!!

SHES PREJUDICE!! My mom says, look at her face, remember it!! Remember, because one day, knowing that look can save your life!!"

My mom insisted I take another look at the old lady, so then I turned to look at the lady again, and tried to remember very well every detail of what that look meant. Unfortunately, that look I recognized long after, and seen that look more and more often throughout my life. I know the looks and hear the awful words they say towards us. I pity those who are prejudice, because they are ignorant and don't know any better. Hate must have been brainwashed into them at infancy. Hate is a nasty infectious plague.

Kay Victorious

My father is a white-passing-Indigenous-person, with deeply internalized oppression, passed down through intergenerational trauma stemming from residential schools...throughout my childhood, he would take me for drives through areas of town with the most homeless people and specifically point out the homeless Native people saying "you wanna end up like those f*ckin OG's ??? You better blah blah blah...Those people are us. They are our relations, they are our family, they are us."

It's taken a very long time for me to be able to take a stand, and not let him carry on spouting his bullshit...and much longer to understand what made him so...vile in my eyes...someday, I hope I can forgive him, and I hope he can find a way to heal...but I can't enable his toxicity by tolerating it. I could never escape it as a child, but now as an adult, there is nothing that can force me to put up with it ever again.

Alice Moon

When I was 10. Drunks were walking by, telling us to go back to the woods to our teepees

Dan VanderGriend

Wagon Burner, what they called me in early grade school - Oroville WA. By late grade 6, I had enough and started kicking ass, now they all call me by my first name or last.

Michael Oshkabewisens

My first time leaving the reserve without my parents, I went to bible camp and everyone made fun of my accent.... then the white camp counselors beat me up in the rooms and stomped on my chest till I couldn't breathe.

Maura Hanaran

Age 9, when my dark-skinned brother got called a racist name and my questions about that word got a strange reaction from my father.

Natalie Bisson

Age 4. I came home crying from Kindergarten because they were singing "1 little, 2 little, 3 little Indians", apparently I came home crying and my mom sent me armed with a new song the next day. Principal called my mother a racist. My mother told him "the only thing racist is that song that your teacher sang that sent my daughter home crying." They never did play that song again.

Casey Key

I got called a prairie n****r at the skatepark by some older kids. Didn't know what the word meant, or why I was a prairie one.

Elly Tamaria

Been experiencing racism all my life, my first was when I was 17 got called a squaw lol.

Yvette Tworabbits

When I was 5. A man yelled at us when my mom took us to the zoo.

Linda Fournier

When I was about 22, some old bitter woman called me a squaw, because I reported her daughter to the board - mainly because she was screaming and yelling as well as throwing stuff and hitting walls all hours of the night.

Lynn Reno

I was adopted into a white family and I am from Lakota Sioux Rosebud reservation South Dakota. The children in school called me ape, monkey and crazy, growing up in Jackson Wyoming. I knew I was different early on.

Amanda Spanish

At the age of 6 or 7 I believe, I went to a Catholic school and they would call me dirty Indian and make the noise with hitting their mouth, you know (fake war whoops).

Nicole Noel

I was 4/5 years old. I was at a gas station with my dad, some old white guy was yelling racial slurs at him and being nasty. I didn't even realize what was happening, I just heard the old guy yelling and I didn't know why he was mad.

So I crawled over to my dad's side of the truck (no carseats then), and looked out his window (it was rolled down) to see what was happening.

My dad just ignored him and chuckled as he pumped gas, which was also confusing, because I just didn't know what was going on.

Then I saw the old guy grab a shovel and start walking, like he was going to hit my dad upside the head from behind, so I climbed out of the truck really fast and started screaming really loud.

I can't remember what happened next, just the moments from when I first realized there was a "problem" to the moment when I was standing in the parking lot screaming and screaming.

Aly Haudley

In 2nd grade, after I'd transferred from a reservation school to a public school in a city, I was told by a li'l white girl that she didn't want to play with me, because I was Mexican (she assumed I was). I didn't know nothing about hating on skin color, and I was not taught either.

Gloria Jan

Around age 3/4 my grandma and I were walking back from bingo one night when a truck full of white men yelled "dirty Natives!" out their window. I was too young to even know what they said and my grandma yelled back "f*ckin a**holes!"

And that was the first time I swore, lol, I copied what she said and said "yeah f*ck you're a**holes!" It's one of those things I've always remembered. Asked my grandma about it years later, and she explained what happened.

Dovie Mute

When I was just 3yrs old at preschool, my teacher called me names, pulled my hair, or ear, or arm, to pinch or grab me.

Shayla Burgis

Probably last year. I was sitting in one of my classes and the guys around me found out I was Native and, every time I'd speak, he would tell me to shut up, because I had no right to speak. Or tell me to go home. And mock my Language by not actually speaking it, but rudely mock it. And mocked my chief. I told him to f*ck off before I show him my Native side, and beat the shit out of him. I haven't heard from him since.

Val Maureen

Kids at school called me Wagon Burner, I didn't understand till I got older. After I realized what it meant, I beat them all up.

Olivia Rose

When I was 4th or 5th grade and my best white friend's mom wouldn't let me in her house to play.

Panda Tallis

I'm half Asian and half Native American. I experienced racism in 4th grade, a white girl made a false accusation against me and the Principal was white. I didn't get to talk and speak for myself, I was silenced. I ended up getting expelled.

Malynda Cosen

I was at a parade in Scottsdale and the sherriffs were shaking all the little kids' hands, except me and my sister. We were the only brown people in the crowd. I felt so bad, and I guess that's why I don't really respect the boys in blue.

Stephanie Bear

Gallup, NM: Eating at a place called Avalon's with my mom in 1998. Two white guys were there saying "Kill all Navajos!" I got into a confrontation with them.

Linda ManyGuns

When I was five, a bully always went after me, and one day I stood up to her and pushed her down. Her mother was near and called me a Black Bastard. I never realized till that moment that I was a different color. I ran home to look in the mirror to see if I was black.

Ivan Longcrow

High School, we went to a basketball game and afterwards went to a place to eat. They flat out told us that they didn't serve our kind. And we needed to leave.

Lex Smitt

When I was in grade eight, I was in our recourse room, and one of the white boys asked me to tell my grandma (the school's Native Language Teacher) in the next room to shut up, because he didn't understand her. Absolutely nothing was done, or said.

Nya George

When I was 15, I moved back to my hometown and quickly realized how we were treated. Couldn't walk into a store without having someone follow you around. First time I was actually aware of my skin color.

Shronda Sarver

7th grade. Went to school in Pheonix, and a white boy called me a squaw....ONE time is all it took, rearranged his face and he never called me that again.

Camille Miller

Kindergarten, "dirty stinkin' Indian".

Kateri Danforth

I was in 2nd grade and a group of white kids circled around me at recess time and danced. using powwow-inspired (phony) chants. It was my first day at that school, some memories never leave your mind. I'm very protective of my children and stand up for anti-bullying at their school.

Chelsea LaDuke

In grade school, being half white and half Native wasn't easy. I was too Native for the white kids, and too white for the Native kids.

Megan Ross

I have light skin, so not many people know of my Indigenous background. In junior high, this girl named Rachelle, when she overheard me talking to my friends, she called me "a filthy savage". I don't know what her deal was, but after that, no one wanted anything to do with her. She then started telling people that she was Indigenous, too.

Kara Hazen

I remember being made fun of in elementary school, too young. In high school, I got called a spear chucker.

Candace Macauley

First time was when I was in grade school. Our principal (in a reserve school) said "most of them savages can't be educated they're too set in their ways."

Norma LaDuke

Second grade was my first major confrontation. When my baby sister was in line at the water fountain, the jr. high school jock pushed her and told her "To the back of the line you dirty injun squaw!"

That's all it took for me. I was a major tomboy raised by 6 older brothers, already in trouble at home for hitting my brother between the eyes with a hatchet. I took all my rage out on that white jock! He never spoke to us again. It was worth suspension for people to know he got his ass kicked by a 2nd grader. And it was even worth the beating I took when I got home by my mixed blood mother.

Eric Brascoupe'

Non aggressive racism ... was 6-7 playing soccer at the local school

Aggressive racism ... High-school sports

Sarah TG

I was in the 3rd grade, had my hair in my typical long braid, bullies laughed at me, and asked me why my hair was so long and always in a braid, because it made me look like "an Indian" (my skin looks white) I admitted that I was part Native, which was met with heavy laughter. They walked away and I thought it was over until my gut instinct told me to turn around, when I did I saw the bullies holding my braid with one hand and a pair of scissors with the other going for my braid! I snatched the scissors and told them if they came near me with scissors again I was going to take those scissors and stab them right through the eye.

They told me it was "just a joke" and that I "look white, so I need to act like it" whatever that means, they tattled on me to the teacher, the white male teacher didn't care about my side of the story at all, he gave me detention and my bullies got nothing! That was my first time ever being sentenced to detention, for defending myself and refusing to "act white."

Elana Faries

In elementary school, my teacher always put the brown kids (and the one white kid from the Rez) in the corner, and/or we would always be each other's partners. Mainly because "brown and white don't mix well", according to her answer, when I first asked why my group of friends were always paired together.

Nicole Trav

I was 2 or 3, my grandpa would take us for ice cream in town. At DQ, the worker told him to "get those little redskins out." I've always been called the N-word in grade school or Beaner/Wetback everywhere I've lived, from Indiana to Colorado. There have been some good people few and far between. This is Amerikkka!

Jolene Saddleback

When I was 5yrs old, my mom and dad were on the verge of divorce, so my mom moved us to Calgary in a woman's shelter. We lived near downtown and there was a school nearby. The school was all white students. They all picked on me, even the teachers were very mean to me, so I told my mom I didn't want to go to school, and she asked me why, so I told her. She then went to the school and raised hell, she even called them out on their racism and they became all apologetic because the school had a "reputation" to keep.

Gina Pelletier

At 1o years old I lived with my foster parents in a well-to-do area, in Winnipeg, Manitoba. I was the only Native girl, besides 1 other boy. I was not invited to hang out with other kids. However, I became passionate about human rights and have taught others about discrimination. It is strange when try to explain to a white person racism, they often deny it's there. See what is happening in the world today.

Rachael Mescher

In grade school I was invited for a sleepover. My friend's dad came home, saw me, and said "no dirty little Indian squaw" was going to stay at his house. I was 8.

Patricia Ramsdell

When a pickup truck of us went to town at the A&W, for ice cream, they wouldn't bring us anything. Some guys yelled at us. My older cousins drove us kids back home. I didn't understand.

Zena Aviles

When my white father told me I'm just like 'them'.

Helen Ross

Has always been in our lives, residential school, genocide, took our language and culture. Schools, from some of the teachers there, seemed to want us to disappear. Business, by the looks we got, some not of same culture as us, could get very vocal. Seemed to think they could say whatever they wanted to us. At Christmas we were at a restaurant, police called, my niece got scared and ran, had to calm her down, if she ran he might of drawn his gun, she was innocent of wrong behavior, as I believe we were. But if we are not the same color as police, they take the side of their same color, in my opinion. At times feels as if we have to defend ourselves, gets tiresome, but we still stand

Danielle Deschenes

When I was 8 years old, I befriended a girl at school and her parents said she couldn't be my friend, because I was Native.

Rachel Abby

When I invited a girl from my class to a birthday in grade 1-2 and she was the only colored girl in the class. My mom told me never to be mean to anyone so I would always invite everyone to my birthday! This women's mom told my mom that her daughter never had been to a birthday party, and was so excited. It literally broke my heart, being so young.

Trudy Perley

In grade 2 I went to an off-reserve school and the boy was calling me 'Injun', so I shut his piehole real quick, with one punch, and stole his lunch. I got in big trouble for that one, not to mention he was the son of a teacher LMFAO. After that it was racism all year for all us li'l Native kids.

Dakota Wavey

Back when I was a kid, I would make friends with lots of the other kids in our community, and I remember having parents tell their kids to not play with the Indian kids. I even got kicked out of a person's home once cause of it. My aunty told me that I would come home crying a lot 'cause of kids parents told them they couldn't play with me.

Noreen Rasmussen

I was a teenager in Saskatoon. Got a haircut with my mom and we walked out of the shop. When we walked out a person walked by and said "must be welfare time!" It hurt me.

Bryan Olson

In the summer before I started grade 5 a boy told my cousins "get off my swings you damn dirt Indians." Suffice to say, I wasn't happy, and that boy learned really quick that even if I'm pale, Anishnabe is in my blood.

Sophia Alcasas

My bro and I ended up being the only brown kids in our elementary school. We didn't learn racism. We didn't know the way they were treating us was wrong. It wasn't until middle school, that kids told us we were being called Beaners because our dad looks Mexican.

Yolanda Shot Both Sides

I was called a Squaw, I was really hurt, and at the same time I was confused.

Maia Satterlund

Headstart, I couldn't go to my white friend's birthday party.

Cole Wytiuk

When I went to culture camp on my reserve. Because I am fair, I was bullied relentlessly for being there. I have since discovered there is racism on both sides, there is a cycle of hate, and you need to find those that accept you for who you identify as.

Mat'iyat Redstar

When a Christian man tried to explain to me that my people were brought here. And then called me an atheist for not believing him.

Connie Haumpey

First grade. I'm Mexican and Kiowa. So the Mexicans didn't accept me and neither did the Natives. Do you know how horrible it is to be a little kid and experience something like that? But because of THAT!! I AM ME AND I LOVE ME!!!

Tommy Brown

My step mom used to hit me every day with spatulas and pans... whatever she could find..... my dad never believed me, with bruises all over my face and hands.... said my mom was a dirty Indian... never said anything about me, just beat me in the morning, around lunch time, and before bed...... going to school was my sanctuary, even though I was failing.....

Rickisha Bear

In Kindergarten, little white boys would pull my braids, and told me I should cut my braids off. They would jump around me doing that thing with their hand and their mouth, mocking powwow music.

Another time I remember is when I was in 4th or 5th and another group of boys came up to me and called me a prairie n****r, which at the time I've never heard those words before. Since I'm Cree, my eyes are very slanted, they used to be mean about that, too. I got told to go back where I came from, which never made sense to me, because even in the history books you'll always see Native Americans.

Allie Morris

Grade school. I got called Sh*t Skin, and some douche bag kid sang "1 little 2 little 3 little Indians."

Kim Whitehead

Grade school, I didn't know what was happening, why they were treating me the way they were, nor how to report it without sounding ridiculous all the time.

"They won't let me play with them", or "That girl looks at me the wrong way". It was subliminal. Even from Métis kids that embraced their white side to fit in.

Lindi Pigeon

At age 4, was told if I didn't like it, I could go live in the woods and eat bugs like the rest of the Indians. 4th grade teacher, in front of entire class felt the need to call out my darker color of skin in the folds of my knuckles, saying my hands are filthy, and made me walk to sink and scrub hands in front of class. The list goes on, but yeah, the early years.

Channelle Beaumont

Grade 1 is my first experience that I remember, I had a friend's parent look at me and my twin sister and tell us her daughter would never come to our house, because we lived on a reservation.

Shiloh Marion

School.... bus driver gave only me a hard time, every day.

Aurora Rodriguez

4th grade I was told I need a shower because I looked "dirty." My favorite is when I was told "Indians aren't allowed to have TV's!"

Nanci Robertson

My white cousins call me a dirty Indian. My Native side of the family call me a fake Indian, or worse. My father was half Cherokee and half Irish. My mother is full German. I am who I am. I love the ones who love me, and avoid the rest.

Nitomac Skush

Walking in school and this white guy called me Chief. I pray for that mf everyday...maybe he'll get right.

Jessica Marie

I was called a minority a lot in middle school, and my ex boyfriend's mom would call me a bunch of names when she got drunk. Kids taunted me in elementary school.

Kevin Laborgne

3rd grade we were studying Native American history. I was a new student, told the teacher that I was Native and came from a reservation, she made me stand up in front and she told the class that I was Native and to ask me questions if they wanted to know anything. At lunch break everyone in my class was telling me "you dont look Native", 'cause I look like a typical white male ('cause my father is Russian), "you dont dress like one", and to show them pictures of my tipi.

I told them that I dress normally and live in a normal house and that it wasn't a tipi, but a longhouse we used to have back in the old days. I got beat up and it went throughout the whole year, and my teacher was always putting me in detention, saying "my people" were disgusting and all kinds of things like that.

I went to see the Principal one day, and he told me to stop being a baby, so I dealt with it till grade six and I learned mix martial arts ever since. I take shit from no one, but have been in a lot of trouble 'cause of it.

Amelia Ward

I transferred to a white school and was the only Native. I was really popular at first, until about 6 months in, it all stopped and turned to silent racism. I assume their parents learned there was a "dirty Native" in their class and "warned" them how "violent" I was, because people were scared I was gonna hurt them, but I never did anything before for them to think that.

Chuck Cromwell

I am from a small town in Alberta (now living in Nova Scotia). I am half Black. This town consisted of whites and Indigenous people and maybe a handful of Blacks. While living in this town I personally only experienced racism towards me once in high school, by an outsider who attended our school for a short time. However I seen racism towards the Indigenous people at a very young age, and until I was educated I have to admit I was one of the ones who were racist towards the Natives. For that I am sorry! I personally never experienced racism towards me until I moved to the Maritimes, where I was educated on racism and bigotry first-hand.

Keyton Warwick

I moved from south Dakota to Ohio, they asked if we still lived in teepee. Teacher said "no, they have trailer housing." lmao 5th grade.

Rebekka Renberg

Grade 1 wasn't allowed to dance. because I was lighter than all the other kids. It's a big thing in my town you're not Metis if you're skin doesn't show it, meanwhile my little sister is as dark as can be, and we have the same parents.

Alexis Alexander

Pretty sure it was when I was in gr.5. Went to a white school for the first time and the girls from gr.6 would look at us in a weird way and the boys would give us dirty looks and rough on us while we played tether ball or soccer. But I always defended myself and whoever I hung out with (another Native). Crazy we experienced racism so young. Why do white people teach their kids to hate at a young age?

Marlies Watters

11 years old in history class, they were talking about the plains wars, my dad was in army (I lived in Missouri at the time). One of the kids leaned forward and said "too bad they couldn't kill all of them, so I wouldn't have to be in class with someone like you."

Went through it a second time in high school I was already treated like sh*t because we lived in an anti-military town in Oregon, got insulted when my dad came and picked up from school a girl looked up racial slurs and kept spitting them out at me the following day.

Melody Hines

Grade 4 when the teacher wanted me to spell the N-word on the black board for spelling test. I would not, and cried in front of the class. I told my mom, who is white, and she took me with her, to find the teacher ... my mom gave her a talking-to and slapped her across the face, and said "my daughter better not have any problems with you or the school cause I'll be back with her Dad."

Jessie Kilgore

Middle school. I grew up with all the kids in my class, it wasn't until all of us kids got into middle school where one of my white friend's father worked as our history teacher. His dad (our teacher), told him he couldn't be friends with me or any of the Native American children, because We were "bad". I wasn't bad. I was brown. He wasn't allowed to be friends, or be caught hanging out with ANY of us Native American kids, because he had a prejudice against us all gang affiliated? Like c'mon!!! We were young innocent children. Not gang bangers!!!

Also, the school tried to suspend a Native student, because he wore his favorite colored red t-shirt every day, all because it was presumed to be gang-related. Us Natives got very upset at the thought of them taking away someone's right to an education because of their favorite color! That next day, every Native American student wore red to represent our dignity and pride. Not for hatred. I grew up on a reservation, so my local school had a LOT of Natives. We were all hated at that school, and punished for things other kids wouldn't normally get punished for. We all grew up feeling like we were bad. I know for myself that, after so many years of being treated like I was bad, I in turn behaved badly because Of how angry and upset I was. I am proud of who I am now, my skin, my heritage and my upbringing.

Colton George

One that sticks out, is me being around 13, pulling my status card out for a $1.00 tax break. The woman rolled her eyes, while I was paying she was looking my card up and down. I forgot it was expired by 1 day... literally 1 day, the woman, after I had my payment approved, noticed that date and immediately said Something along the lines of "oh too bad, we have to do it over again"... now thinking about it as an adult, I had every right to walk out. But my confused-ass did it again anyway. Or my exes step dad, farmer guy from a little town. Gives all of his family nicknames... mine was "colt".... as in the brown colt cigars... I'd love to run into his old ass again LOL

Nicole Edmund

From what I remember THE FIRST TIME I experienced racism and knew that that's what it was, grade 4 ... maybe. One kid at school on lunch hour and 3 kids on my block. I couldn't understand why they were mean to me, all I knew is that I felt less than.

Kira Honson

2nd or 3rd grade, they called me and a couple other kids Savages, and some other shit they shouldn't have been saying at that age. Ended up stabbing a kid in the hand with a pencil in 4th grade for calling me *"timber n****r"*.

Shawanoqueaashiik Ojaanimigiishickook

Grade 3 was the worst, I got sent to the Principal's office for stating Native Americans were here first. But kids from grade 1 up noticeably chose not to hang out with me, based on my skin color, I guess. Although the ones who did, stood by my side then. and continue to. I experienced brown on brown racism because I was "white washed." Too brown for the whites, too white for my own. Racism all around sucks and it's a scary world for our future generations!

Dawn Teller

2nd grade learning to read" No dogs or Indians allowed", outside of most places in my hometown.

Marc Pandza

Grade 2 my teacher pointed out I was an Indian and said I would be a good boy if I washed my face and combed my hair. My mom kept me clean and I had a brush-cut short hair. I wasn't embarrassed, I was mad.

Krista Marie

I look back and when I was little my hands and feet were red, my adoptive white family would show friends and relatives my "Red Indian skin."

Michelle Charity

My whole life. My dad hated other races but our own... I heard racial slurs growing up and I didn't understand why.

Charles McGrath

The first time I went to school after moving from Florida to the Rez in Michigan. I was in kindergarten and the kids kept pulling on my hair. The teacher had the nerve to say "if you don't want 'em messing with it, cut it off."

For being so young, I was so angry for it. I just wanted to slap her, however I moved to the rez school left those crackers in that busted wrapper.

Stella Anderson

I'm an urban Native growing up in Phoenix and Tucson, but I could remember when I went to either of my grandparents reservations for vacation and going to the Rez border towns and experiencing racism, especially in Casa Grande, Winslow, and Flagstaff. Now I'm in the UK, where my husband works for US Dept of Defense, and the only racism I've experienced is on the military bases, not the British run bases. Brits have their own racism, but it's not directed at minorities from the US. They are more sympathetic and knowledgeable about our history, or they are willing to learn. A remark I sometimes make is "I've come to live in the land of my conquerors", and I see uneasy laughs. It makes me feel good!

Carolynn Dawson

Grade 4, being made fun of, saying I had bugs in my hair. Making fun of my clothes. Because my dad lost his job.

Lesley Fisher

As a kid, it was bad that I tried to wash the brown off my skin.

Melissa Lewis

I took my kids out to eat at a restaurant here in Anchorage. There was a woman and her husband asking the waitress to "move them away from me and my kids", my kids asked me why they were mad at us! I just said, I don't know God will punish them for not liking us, don't worry just eat and be happy.

Alexis Wabasse

I was told to kill myself because I am Indigenous, I get called Brown Skin Girl almost every day by "friends", and I go to my white friend's house, her parents said "don't bring dirty Indians in the house!"

Shannon Ernest

Age9, I think..when I was called a Wagon Burner by my school teacher,.before he made me eat looseleaf paper, "damn wagonburners dont listen"

I told my mom it was some kid in my class. I didn't even know what he was upset about because I never burned wagons before.

Marie Fontaine

At 5. A girl lived close to our school and took me to her house, her mother looked at me with disgust and told her daughter not to bring dirty little Indians home. I forgot all about this until I remembered how old I was. I took off on my brothers and thought I made a friend and I was so happy she invited me over. I was Native and poor, but I was never dirty. Sad thing was, it didn't hurt or bother me, how this lady acted, but I lost a friend. That hurt.

Vicki Soto

I guess it was about kindergarten because I went to a predominately white school, and then my mom would take me to the rez and get dropped off at my other grandma's. She was pure 100% Cheyenne Native, and the whole clan I would wonder why they were so dark and lived in a little shack with a wood-burning cook stoves and always smelled of burnt wood. And ate drymeat and potatoes,.then get picked up on the Sunday evening to go home and take baths to go to school the next day. With a whole different band of people that lived a whole different life. It was confusing at first till I got use to my grandma, with her traditional dress and walking cane and playing in the dirt with one rag doll. As she would sit there watching, talking in Cheyenne, and smiling. I miss her now, she lived till her 90's. R.I.P.

Branden King

Grade seven, kids found out I was half Blackfoot, didn't matter they danced around taunting me, with ignorant chants.

Kyle Nezstosie

I was about in kindergarten. Went to a white friend's house, he came out and said his parents won't let him play with me because I was "brown".

Victor Isaac

I must have been about 7, my brother 9, we went to a diner and we had to sit in the back. I never understood why, and my brother explained years later.

Victoria Paton

Preschool. The kids would call me a half breed, they refused to go near me and I was bullied in the change room and they would shove me into the water. I was always afraid to leave my mother, I would hug her at the door. Or I'd rush to get into the change rooms first so I could avoid them.

Ruby Dawn Manning

2nd grade in Carson City on the school bus. Had all summer in the swimming pool. Boys on the bus called me "Little Ni**er Girl" relentlessly.

Heidi Blackrabbit

Not the first but the most memorable was when my 11th grade history teacher said "what happened to the Native people wasn't genocide."

Winona Haylee

Grade 4, my crush called me a squaw.

Jennifer Spence

In child and family services. My foster parents physically abused us, called us dirty Indians. Threw hard objects at us. Wouldn't let us participate in games. The list goes on. Fed us different meals, apart from the family - ages 6 to 8.

Shondyl Johns

1982 I was in grade two. And a boy who was a friend previously, made fun of me for being Métis. I beat him up at recess, because I could. He never made fun of me again.

Abbey Jacobs

7th grade when a guy I had a crush on made fun of my tribe's religion, and of me for being from a "poor" reservation.

Lloyd Abraham

In Immaculata school here in Burns Lake, we had to walk down a gully, as soon as we got to the bottom we got pelted with rocks from both sides, and to top it off, we got strapped at school for being late.

Leigh Ashlie

My worst case was when I was 10, I moved from the Rez and had an accent. Had "rezzy vibes", didn't wear what the kids were wearing. A bully found me and picked on me for years. He made me hate myself. I never told my mom. I was strong. I felt I could handle it. Anyway, he turned a bunch of kids on me. And I had no friends for awhile after that, I became a loner. And I never complained about it. I would have like a couple friends here and there. I would make friends with all the other Natives. Lol. That's what you get for living in an suburban area. Also the Natives would always leave, so my friends always came and left. I found out later that the boy who bullied me was part Native. You would never guess, blue eyes, blonde hair. I'm an adult now and I feel bad for him, he was probably picking on me for the part he hated about himself.

Susie Hagan

I was 23 or 24 and was at gas station and a guy and his girlfriend made the HOW sign at me, then laughed!

Beth Veltrano

I was 10 year's old in a public pool (we went to Tennessee to meet my mom's 2nd husband's family), and I went to climb up the stairs to get out, and my hand grabbed the rail the same time as a little blonde girl. She pulled her hand quickly away and said "ewww, don't touch me you burnt biscuit!"

Davonte Hinojosa

When I was a kid, I used to get pulled over and patted down just for being "on the wrong side of town", every time I went to visit my friends or family. I used to walk down the streets with my brother, and people would yell n****r. Parents of people I knew used to call us "the Mexicans". This went on from age 6 to at least 18. By then, people hid their racism because they know most people don't accept it now, and don't want their image ruined.

David Mata

From what I remember clearly on my own, Catholic school, kindergarten. But it started way before then. My mother is a tribal member, but could pass for white. Strangers would either shame her for being "white", and having an Indian baby, or ask her where she got me. I guess we are just born into it.

Stephi Etsitty

Kindergarten/1st grade. We lived in Durango CO. My baby sitter Debby, and her daughter Kia, would treat me different than the other kids. They were so mean to me. I used to cry & wait by the front door until my mom come for me every evening.

Kia (who about 15 or 16) was supposed to walk me all the way to my classroom/trailer, but she would only walk me to the end of their trailer park. I still had at least 5 blocks to go. One time it had just snowed & everything was frozen. It was time to go to school. Struck me as odd, we took a different way to school that day. Well turns out she lead me to the middle of the frozen pond, pushed me down & told me "I hope u Indians know how to swim! Better get your red Indian ass to school!"

Then she took off back to her trailer. I got up real slow & inched my way off that pond. I cried as I walked in the snow all the way to school, because my foot went thru the ice, my brand new shoes got wet & it was freezing cold.

They called my mom & asked why I had wet shoes & why was I so late to school. I told my mom what happened. When my mom went to Debby to confront her & her daughter, Kia lied to her mom and said that I ran off from her towards the pond, and that I tripped over a log & got wet.

I don't know what my mom said or did, but after that day I never had to go back. I had a new babysitter named Hope. She also had a daughter & they were so much nicer. I never wanted to leave, lol. But that same school, all the white kids would call me Injun ... Pocahontas ... Redskin ... Dirty NDN ... Prairie N****r ... squaw ... so many other names.

Ravonda Swimmer

When I was 12 years old, my sister had a bi-racial baby. The man who owned the land we lived on threw rocks at my sister's car, with my niece in the back. He kicked us out and we had to move. Now every kid in our family is bi-racial. My kids are enrolled Eastern Band Cherokee. They have experienced racism in school. My daughter was called a savage, so my son went to school and jumped on that boy. My son was called the N-word and told to go back to the reservation.

Tamara Edgars

Racism was bad in high school. The beginning of the year, white people in front of the school said "Oh the Indians are already showing up."

Desaray Glen

A month ago, an older lady came thru my drive-thru and she said "did you do a dance, can you do another to stop all this rain. Or is that how it works?"

Marcel Meekis

All my life, but the one that sticks with me is, when I was in grade school. This older white boy tells me to come over and tells me "not to play on playground". I was wondering why, but I still played on it. So he just confronts me, I stood up for myself, and I get into trouble.

Melissa Freeman

When I was in 6th grade, although not from someone white but Mexican, he started patting his mouth and chanting "woo woo woo woo", so I started singing "La cucaracha" at him, and mocking how Mexican people dance. I made him laugh, then I laughed, and we became friends.

Tatanka Wanbli

Third grade in Rapid City, South Dakota ...was called prairie n****r. Then watching the Indians play baseball, fans doing the tomahawk.

Denise Desjarlais

I experienced racism when I started school, my so called teachers were supposed to be there to teach me how to read, write, and arithmetic, but I was treated with disrespect. The slaps to my face, the slaps on my hands, the insults, the crackers and cod liver oil I was forced to swallow; and the horrific times we had to stand and listen to God Save The Queen, and listen to the Principal talk about himself, and then force my cousin, who is left handed, to use his right hand, and he would cry because it hurt. These are only some stories I remember. There are many more stories I can tell but nobody listens.

Toshia Cook

When I was in 5th grade. I went to a birthday party. A boy said "why did you invite her, she's a nasty Indian. I didn't let that Nahola "white" bother me. That was 1985.

Maye Maye

When I was 12yrs old at Sacred Heart Catholic school, an old French teacher humiliated me, because I did not know how to speak French! And made me cry! And as soon as my mother found out, she marched to the school, and made that teacher cry, in front of everyone, and asked her how did she like it?

Royale WMS

1997 at an Edmonton Oilers game, we were just kids, attacked by an older couple calling us dirty Indians and such. I'll never forget that.

Bailey Toulouse

I remember being an 11 year old kid, on a house league hockey team playing for C, could've been D division, but anyways near the end of the game we're beating a team 7-3, and a kid comes out of nowhere hits one our players. Then a brawl happened, penalties and what not, then as it's all getting sorted out, players are getting put in the box.

Then a coach from the other team says "Don't go get your tomahawks for a weapon!"

I remember hearing that, and I was tearing up about ready to cry on the ice, then a whole lot of shouting happened between the benches and the other Native parents yelling. After the game, I heard the guy who said it, had to get escorted out and it was their home rink.

Cody Hansen

When I was 6/7, teacher would slap my hands with a meter stick if I wasn't sitting straight enough. I was one of the few Natives in the class, so she singled me out. Been dealing with it ever since.

Mark Romero

1959, when I was in 2nd grade. Playing tag and I was IT. I was chasing a little white girl that I liked and she turned around, stopped me in my tracks, and said, "I can't play with you because my mom and dad said your family is a bunch of dirty Indians."

Becky Churchill

In a community when I was very young, just walking through a trailer park with my cousin. A white woman and her twin daughters gave us look of disgust. Then every year K - 10th grade. Had to fight again for them to stop the taunting during my sophomore yr. Raised in a white community.

Crystal Salas

When I was 3 1/2 years old, two white cops called my mother a dirty Indian and pulled and dragged her by her hair.

Ryan McDonald

Elementary: age 6/ grade 1, from teachers. Moving into grade 7, I tried signing up for Extended French as second language, since the provincial government forced us to learn it, as Native languages weren't available at the time, but yeah long story short: I was told to "stick to your own language" and the teacher was mean. And this was a public school in a small town.

Penny Lawrence

Elementary School walking home a kid was trying to upset me by fallowing me and yelling "Pocahontas!"

Adeline Large

In elementary school. Was called a "stupid squaw" by a white boy. I gave him a bloody nose, lol.

MaryElyn Eaglebear

I remember one day after school, while waiting for the bus we would play at the park for a couple minutes. I made a white friend, and we started playing, but then her parents came and told her not to play with me because I was a "Savage."

I didn't know what that meant until I got home and I asked my mom. She hugged me and told me not to listen to them. She was so mad, I didn't understand what the problem was until I got a bit older.

Omar Thomas

First grade when my brother was getting beat by a group of white kids. In return I beat most of them up and I got kicked out of school for fighting, but the white kids were not in trouble for it.

Rathan Neece

I was in a little town in Nebraska, playing baseball, and a group of white kids came over to me and started calling me a "dirty Indian", and other stuff. I was about 12-13.

Robin Laverne

I was 4 or 5 playing, out in our neighborhood, my little friend was stung by a bee and asked me to go to her house (we lived in townhouses). We arrived and she was crying, but told them that I was an "Indian, but a nice one!" I had to wait by the door.

Loretta BlackBuffalo

Most of my life with slurs and what not, but the worst was when I was jumped just for being a Native. The girls I lived with wanted to fight back, but I let it go. I let the Creator handle that mess.

Amanda Blanche

When I was told, I looked dirty on my arms. I went to wash it off but they said I can't wash off my skin. I was six.

Susanna Elsworth

Yeah, around 1973, 5th grade, these girls & their mother said some very racist things about my friend, who is Native. They would throw things at us & tried to dump water on us. Long story short, they grew up to be assholes, while my friend & I are still very good friends.

Jody Dawn

When I was 5, my brother (from foster home I was raised in) came into the bathroom and said "you are an Indian" and I remember feeling shame ... and not for being naked in the bath tub. Until that moment, I thought that was my family, I didn't know I wasn't, or that I was different from them, but from then on I never felt like I belonged. I'm healed now and connecting with my Indigenous culture.

Asher Skulls

Trick or treating with my cousin and 2 uncles. Bunch of white guys in a truck stopped and said "f*ck Indians!" Then laughed and threw candy at us, then drove off. I was 7 years old. They looked like college or high school preps. My uncles laughed at them and were ready to throw down. But I very much remember that.

Cheyanna Thomas

My parents always told me, it's okay to be proud of your culture just don't advertise it. Especially because I look more like my dad (white) and I could "get away with it". To me that was the beginning of racism for me.

Angelina Fernandez

Starting from a very young age, 4 or 5 years old. Other children my age would call me "Red Indian." Where else would they learn that from - other than parents, siblings, auntie, uncle, cousins and even grandparents?

Tyrell Kakakeway

Grade 7, my parents finally let me transfer to a school mostly dominated by Caucasians. While I was in math class me, the other people of color were separated from the white students, and put into different a classroom without an explanation. I proceeded to hear certain kids talk to each other, usually referring to us with racial remarks. It didn't last long, but certainly left an impression.

Christina Renaud

Kindergarten. A boy called me a "Wagon Burner", and the teacher thought it was hilarious. I asked my mom what that was, and all I know is, my grandparents went to the school, and suddenly I was in another class.

Chastity Stamp

As a Native woman. I would say it first happened in Play School from a teacher in Edmonton Alberta. In kindergarten, I had rocks thrown at me in a playground, because I was a Native, just trying to have fun and play.

Murray Sanderson

Grade one, the white kids would say "the Indian school bus is coming", then they would go inside and leave school yard empty, while I waited for my friends.

Leah Durbin

High school, I was moved to the city, some white guys threw hot coffee on me at the bus stop. Told me to "go back to my own country!" Umm, my people were here first, dumba**.

Ami Leigh

I don't remember this incident, but my parents always talk about how I came home crying from kindergarten because the kids told me I can't be an Indian, since they were all dead. The first time I remember a specific incident is probably age 6 or 7.

Anita Kirsten

When I was told that I was "only good for beer bottles and babies" in grade 7! Because I wanted to be enrolled in Science and Math!!

Devonee Whiteman

Can't remember but this one experience has stuck with me for years. I was at a friend's house and her brother was extremely racist, to the point where he wanted me out of the house and refused to sit on or touch anything I touched. I was a shy and awkward kid, and that f*cked me up for a long time.

"STARLIGHT TOUR", EVER KNOW SOMEONE WHO HAS BEEN ON ONE?

Question 3

**Starlight Tours" are where police drop you off in a location far from where you were picked up, or far from the city, etc – sometimes in freezing weather: a Maclean's article reveals the details: https://macleans.ca/news/canada/new-light-on-saskatoons-starlight-tours/

**112 people answered with a simple "yes", the following are the more detailed responses:

Aiyela Nighttraveler

My friend josh, he was ok though, he got picked up. He sobered up while walking and made a complaint. But nothing was done.

Nahab G.

A guy in my area (Val d'Or, Quebec) was found dead under a bridge. Last seen being taken by police.

Charley Swan

My mother, and she was pregnant. 2 officers drove her far away from town, took her jacket and told her to walk back. It was close to midnight, sometime in January. The perfect time and place to force a young pregnant woman freeze to death. This is why I will never trust the Canadian RCMP or police force. Murderers of thousands of men, woman, and children – they are protected and will continue to walk free. A trucker saw my mom walking about 5 minutes after the officers left, that's who saved her.

Serity Moon

My brother, who was 17 at the time.

Natalie Bisson

In Toronto. Cherry Beach is where they brought our people.

Troy Wilson

Me, my bro, separate occasions, dropped off out of town. We were threatened with incarnation and beatings. They said, "we have the law out our side, no one will believe 'you', a drunken Indian!"

This was done in the cold of winter, dropped us off about seven miles from the city. They said,"a walk will sober you up, consider this your lucky day", and they drove off.

Clayton Dorsey

Let out of police car 16yrs OLD Downtown Oklahoma, 2a.m. Ran back.

Tara Kielczewski

Yes, it used to happen to my cousins all the time.

Jasmine St. Amand

Never happened to me, but I do know it still happens in Thunder Bay.

Tito Ottis

I was once at 15 years old but was picked up by the OPP, lol, it was the city police department that dropped me off, and was the provincial police picking me up 25 mins later, lol.

Patricia Nekyathap

24 years ago we lost my best friend, found in the outskirts of Saskatoon, Saskatchewan - due to the starlight tour. He was the greatest, my daughter was so close to him, called him "Uncle". He nicknamed her 'My Smurfette'. To this day, she still misses him as we all do.

Nikki Nahnepowisk

My dad used to go on a lot of them, Regina Police Service knew him very well, even took his shoes at one time, he still survived.

Jenna Beattie

My husband was picked up and brought to the Algonquin reserve (he's Ojibwa) in the middle of the night, and left in a place where he didn't know anyone, and wasn't from.

Ashley Severight

My dad's friend. I recently found out that my grandma was taken for a tour as well. She passed away when I was young, way before I even knew about them.

Mabel Nipshank

A lot in my area - brothers cousins, friends. It happens a lot in Alberta and Saskatchewan during the winter. Also they take their shoes and jackets.

Star Cardinal

Yes, more like rides to random places, it happens a lot, especially to people who need medical attention - then they end up dying where they are dropped off. I personally know of 3, and 1 died.

Sakapeep Randall

I have, in Thunder Bay, Ontario I was out from high school.

Shane Strongman

My buddy got taken to an industrial area in Calgary from Ranchman's, in the cold of January. Good thing he had a cell, he was able to call for a cab home.

Julie Barkman

Yes, just this past February. My cousin's son was taken outside the city and left there to walk back home, took him over 6 hours to get to his moms. (Winnipeg, MB.)

Sharon Peluso

Many years back, my son was taken 5 miles out of Westlock, AB to walk back. RCMP have been doing this for years and getting away with it.

Brenton Disbrowe

I knew of someone that happened this to him, he was pan handling.

Andrew Jolicoeur

I know at least 2 or 3 people I've met or worked with. What's more f*cked is how Saskatchewan RCMP and Saskatoon Police keep taking the starlight tour comments off of their equality posts.

Virginia Yellowface

Yes, 2 men from my rez, Lawrence Wagner who died, and Darrell Night, who lived to tell his story.

Van Day

Neil Stonechild (a widely publicized victim of a Starlight Tour), was a friend of many of my friends. I never hung out with him, but I know lots who have back in Saskatoon where I grew up.

Bailey Campbell

My cousin and her friends were dropped off outside of town by police, when they were teenagers drinking.

Dick Smith

A couple of my cousins have. One in Thunder Bay. And another one in Ottawa.

Bridget Conn

My dad.

Ashleigh Lori-Anne

An ex-boyfriend got picked up by Edmonton Police while he was tipsy. They drove around and dropped him off, without shoes, in the middle of winter. He called me in the middle of the night scared, I won't ever forget that call.

William Clayton

My sister's oldest brother, Rodney Naistus, was taken on a starlight tour in Saskatoon. He was found in the snow bank the next day, frozen stiff. It was middle of winter when the RCMP did this.

Tuelot Fraser

One of my uncles just told me the other day that my other uncle use to be taken up the mountains, beaten and left there there. Is that the "starlight tour"? It saddens me that goof cops get away with such cruelty to humans.

Jadzia Crow

My cousin this winter, here in Thunder Bay.

Harlen Crier

My wife's cousin. He's the one who survived and basically exposed it. He moved far from Saskatchewan and WILL not come back. His name is Darrell Night.

Dee McHugh

The head honcho here in this BC town, took my son up the mountain, hog tied him, and threatened to do something to him if he didn't leave town. My son didn't want to provoke any beating or be left in the mountains alone. YES RACISM ALIVE AND WELL IN CANADA! Some Cops think they are judge, jury and executioner!

Rhiannon Edge

Neil Stonechild ...age 17, killed by police, who stole his clothes and shoes in the middle of winter, in Saskatchewan. Death by exposure, he had frozen tears on his face when he was found.

HAVE YOU EVER HAD POLICE AIM THEIR GUNS AT YOU?

Question 4

**412 responses were simply "Yes", below are those that provided more context

Dane Murdock

Yes, cuffed and barrel to back of my head, 'cause I "looked like someone with a warrant."

Kristopher Richard

Yup and I was just a teeny, not even 16 years old yet.

Anthony Sams

Yeah, and heard his young partner in training say "this is cool".

Justin Olmstead

My brother has, on multiple occasions. We grew up in the same house, same city, what separates us in the outside world is that I have white skin, light brown hair and blue eyes and my brother has brown skin, black hair and brown eyes.

Maureen Tammy

Stopped on highway; checked my back pack. Said I "fit a description", and then left.

Ray Williams

Yup. Seattle. Got pulled over and guns drawn the whole procedure, like on Cops or something - turn around, hands on your head, get on the ground.

Sean Speers

I had a bad incident where someone slipped something in my drink, and I tried getting home, only to get stopped by police who refused to help me home, but instead twisted my arms back, while I tried explaining I had shoulder surgery and my arm can't bend backwards.

Crystie Cloud

Yup, with my girls in the back seat.

Hilda Mann

Yes! After a home invasion... because most of us were Indigenous they didn't know the bad guys from the good.

Steve Dumont

Twice, once in Surrey BC and once New Westminster BC.

Stephen Floyd

First time at 13, last at 47

Jane Wesley

6 cops pointed their guns at me for no reason when I was 18.

Eli de Vries

Yes. Standing Rock and Black Lives Matter Protest.

Candace Macauley

Yup, even had them pull me outta the shower, after breaking my door down. And they held my 10 & 3 year olds at gun point at the same time. Now my children are traumatized.

Norman Debassige

Had 6 OPP officers pull up, after non-Natives on Mississagua Rez had made false reports that I was walking around shooting a gun off. 3 cruisers show up, my 2 boys, 3 n 5 years old, had cap guns - toy caps guns. The cops were ready.

Shar Shouting

Yep, I was 16, pinned on the ground and cuffed.

Nicole Renae

Yup when I was 16. A week before this happened, the cops in my area killed a 18 year old on his own front porch, unarmed and was trying to take his wallet out of his pocket. So when we got pulled over a week later, with no particular reason, other than out kinda late, the cops pulled guns out, he asked the driver if he was nervous, my friend said "F*ck yea! You guys just killed one of my best friends last week!" I thought I was going to see my friend get shot right in front of me.

James McMillan

Yes I have had 10 assault rifles pointed at me cuz the lan lord saw a pellet gun and he called the cops. I wasn't afraid, they were trying to scare me, saying I'm not who I say I am, but I stood my ground.

Anita King

Yup, 6 months pregnant the 1st time ... I wasn't even arrested, because I didn't break no law.

Delbert Long

Yes. For no reason, had to lay on the ground.

Kirsty Waskahat

Yes, I was like 14, they thought we were in a stolen car.

Christopher Mt.Pleasant

SWAT had the audacity to point their guns at my 7 year old cousin and asked if he'd ever "looked down the barrel before". Still makes me mad thinkin' about that.

Alan Seegerts

Yup, in La Crescenta,California...9 cops, all w/ pistols

Cici Ryder

I had one tell me to try to make a run for it & be had his hand on his side arm.

Cecile Taylor

Yes. I even had the military surround our car, fully loaded and ready to shoot. Smh. We were unarmed.

Bobby Louis

Shot me with rubber bullets 6x's. Because I was reaching for my wallet in my back pocket.

Mackenzie Rawlake

Cuffed, face/belly down, huge black gun, camo suited up. That smartened me right the f*ck up.

Melissa White

Yup, set their dogs on me, too. I didn't think I could jump so high. I looked like a cat perched on a fence. Turns out somebody had called in saying there was a suspicious woman walking down the alley - I was going home from work.

Sam Malcolm

Yep. It's like a f*cked up right of passage.

Jake Salazar

Plenty of times... Just walking home drunk with whisky bottle in my coat, guess it was a gun, lmao.

Lorin Volden

Yup, lots all at once, during an old fashioned drug raid, lol. We stayed still and did not move as told, was quite different.

April Devine

My uncle (whom passed recently) lived in a neighborhood which consisted of mostly white people, some were racist others, others weren't racist at all. Anyways, this one day my grandma went to go visit him and while they were visiting they hear a cop with a microphone saying my uncles name, and for him to go outside with his hands up, and then they called my grandmas name! My grandma said when she went out there, they had guns pointed straight at her, she said it must've had been like 5 cops with their guns pointed at her. Mind you my grandma is 68, I guess the cops were very rude to her. It was an act of racism, all of it.

I guess what happened was, a racist neighbor called the cops and said my uncle had a gun for no apparent reason!! (He didn't have a gun) and after everything he was evicted, and for what, for being Native and supposedly having a gun.

Hearing this from my grandma broke my heart, because she's an Elder, and the fact the cops had her in their sight with their guns still bothers me today.

Marcus Cory

I had cops aim they're guns at me, while being tasered by 3 other cops at the same time.

Ethaniel Wesley

Yep, when I was 12 and our house was raided. They busted in my room while I was playing Xbox, and three cops had their guns on me. They grabbed me by my shirt and forced me to the ground, but I don't think they realized I was just a lil kid because I'm a tall guy. I was 5"9 when I was 12, still traumatizes me to this day.

Phillip Soop

Yup, dogs and tasered with a shotgun pointing at my head. And after they ID'd me, they realized they had the wrong person.

Budd Yupe

I had guns drawn on me in Vegas - for not having a front license plate.

Rob Blankinship

Yes, more than a few times and its pretty scary when you did nothing wrong but be a Native, in the wrong place at wrong time.

Rachele Toliver

Police surrounding me, screaming "get on the ground" with guns pulled and I was told if I move I'm getting shot, and I was only walking down the street, minding my business.

HOW DO WE PUT AN END TO POLICE BRUTALITY?

Question 5

Christina Renaud

Mental health screenings of perspective officers, cross cultural education. That's just a couple ideas. I don't think that would be the end-all-be-all, but it would probably help.

Cori Dee

Ongoing testing training education and monitoring, cut the racism off at the legs, starting at the top to the bottom. A clean sweep.

Melinda Bain

Dismantle the initial process of hiring. It's outdated and exclusive for people who have never had to survive adversities. This limits diversity and maintains those in power... It's more than just having a random brown person who fits in their structure.

This whole police issue on 'serving' and 'protecting' is only meant for some people under the law and carding or over-surveilling others.

Lily Naytowhow

Better training and education with smaller classrooms.

Strong Walker

By only allowing officers to serve 5 year terms. This will ensure constant turn over, no good ol'boy system, and not let police get burned out and callus.

Linda Bonnefoy

Start enforcing jail time, charges and immediate loss of employment. The cops should be treated harsher than a regular citizen because of the abuse of power.

Ana David

Duty to intervene, hire more social service responders.

Lea Ann

It starts with upper management, then when that morale has changed you'll see and feel it throughout the system. Cultural competency mandatory education and an internal reporting system for police officers to disclose racial bias without retribution. Also we need color on the force....a recruitment and retention strategy to hire Indigenous applicants who meet the requirements!! It all starts with the bureaucracy, if that doesn't change....nothing does unfortunately!

Jude Cruz

This all comes down to money. Reverse any laws preventing monetary compensation for bad policing and wrongful death. Allow punitive damage lawsuits against individual police, city, state and Federal police entities.

Kate Reynolds

Replace a majority of police officers with social workers and other social service providers.

Sophia Peters

Longer training & more protocols.

Luis Reyes

Quality over Quantity when it comes to training. Adhere to current protocols and truly hold everyone accountable for their actions. Transparency at all levels is what it will take.

Ace Godinus

It should be mandatory for them to have and maintain certifications periodically and pass courses /exams in all areas with score of at least 80% percent or higher.

I'd also add that police departments should be investigated for high numbers of complaints where citizens' rights have been violated. Said departments should purge the offending officers and deny them their pensions. Those pensions should go to police brutality victims funding programs and rehabilitation programs for guilty / found to be innocent parolees who have served time for non-violent offenses that are trying to re-integrate back into society. This way, police don't get sued and the communities have to flip the bill, and the old way of policing dies for fear of personal loss.

They should also have to continually train in suspect identification / apprehension / weapons retentions training courses, so they aren't pulling there guns out for every little thing. They should also be held accountable for every action / inaction when it comes to the safety of all communities / citizens they swear to protect.

Further more, law abiding citizens with the proper training, means, and ability should be allowed to practice self defense without fear of police over reaction / prosecution. The safety of the community and police power should not be placed solely on them.

As for the Rez. Those who live in PL280 states or states where police just show up on the Rez, Tribal Government should practice its sovereign power and not allow foreign law enforcement officers on the Rez without Tribal Police escort / oversight.

Stephanie Googoo

No guns and cultural sensitivity and awareness meetings with their local communities. They need to know the unknown and hopefully respect the community they serve and maybe they can redeem themselves and get respect again.

Valerie Greene

Better training to be more compassionate and harsher punishment for incidents.

Cody Hutchinson

The older police standards were very regimented. Lots of discipline and structure. They have gotten so far away from that, the training today has no practical uses in society. They should go back to that, train them to react to a situation. And the recruiting selection should not be eased up, it seems too many racist immature cowards are slipping in to the ranks. Get people that can rely on their training and to not go shooting up people.

Kai Victorious

We abolish the RCMP, create a new policing institution with less funding and focused on more specific issues, and also creating new institutions to address the many roles the current institution of police fill that specialize in serving those specific roles. Also, cracking down on police unions and not allowing them to create immunity for officers is vital. Big measures to accountability are needed at a base level.

Faith Simon

Their requirements should be more elaborate. Need more training, At least 2 years training with human rights as well a select few laws *Pertaining to the public such as stolen goods, public indecency, effective yet non harmful physical education for taking down actual women or men who are a threat. Put into laws that minors, unless threatening with lethal means, should not be handled rough by any means.

Carl Bear

Get rid of cops investigating other cops first of all. Use civilians of all ethnicities and genders to decide the fates of police being questioned for brutality. Overhaul police forces from top to bottom, get rid of known hot head cops by not allowing them to advance in the ranks.

Ronnie Pine

My "Community service" lasted longer than what it takes to become a Police Officer. Something wrong with that. Like what it takes to be a Nurse, RN. Recruits need to be better trained, or some type of degree, to wear the badge of an Officer. Because what we have now, isn't working. AND better screening of recruits.

Tó'aheedlíinii Hastiin

National registry for bad cops making them un-hireable in the 50 states if their listed.

Shayna Alexandria

Disarming them of militarized weapons, cut the funding. World would thrive with community watch and protection. Put that cut police funds into mental health and addiction facilities, make post-secondary education free. Eliminate poverty. We will eliminate police brutality.

Michele Provancial

Those people who want to be law enforcement officers should have psychological testing first as well as a thorough background check on the way they were raised. They must also have training on emotional intelligence as well as conflict management and resolution. Their supervisors must also watch for signs of stress and burnout so they can be taken off the streets for a while. Regardless of good intentions, there really are some heinous individuals out there who can make police officers' Lives a nightmare so it's important the officers have support when they need it.

Dan Shulla

Simple. Let all cops know they will be held accountable. Using a taser on a child will also result in charges of child abuse/assault.

Holli Muck

Do away with qualified immunity and police unions. Fear of consequence is what keeps most in line. Police won't be held accountable with those 2 things still in place.

Jerry Chalifoux

Get applicants to live and train amongst different nationalities.

Curtis Hall

Make the cost of defending these criminal cops come out of their retirement fund! They would start to police themselves as well. Charge them as you or I would be charged for doin the same crime and throw them in general population when in prison.

Sarah TG

Make the police academy 3-4 years long then people will need more than a GED/diploma, 21 days of training and a gun to be a cop! That will weed out the racists that just want a power trip from the people that actually want t dedicate their lives to the community.

Rosemary Caye

Congress needs to conduct an outside study of the entire justice department from the bottom up from an outsource institution and implement changes immediately. They also need to dissolve immunity from the police. A new beginning. Oh they also need an separate oversight committee to oversee them.

Katie Holtsoi

Unfortunately it's a deeply embedded system of racism, those who "hold the power" and abuse it need to unlearn that system. The genesis of the police system is inherently racist too! We say defund because it's a call to take the focus/energy/time/resources away from over policing and put it into programs and orgs to benefit the community in a better and non-violent way. Over policing and incarceration does nothing for a community, and these murders are a vile byproduct of it all. And especially as Native people we have to also unlearn this colonial system that has brought harm to our communities as well. Progress in the right direction will take time, just think about all the anti-racist work of civil rights leaders of the past, even after what they have achieved for Black people and POC, we still deal with new obstacles and age old obstacles every day. I believe education and political action is one of the factors that will help us achieve eradication of violence from police. It's just one of the many ways we can dismantle it, but we also must protest, donate, petition, do the anti-racist work, and hold people accountable for their racism.

AFTERWORD

Rocky and I playing Donkey Kong on my
Colecovision (back in the day)

I was raised by a Black man, from the age of 4, my li'l brother and I.

A Black man whose people are also of the Muscogee (Creek) Nation.

This Black Indigenous man represents our unified struggle.

His name is Ralph Delano Pierce, aka *"Rocky"*

You know what, f*ck the *"right words"* ...

... lemme tell you about this Black Indigenous man

This Black Indigenous man has known the Eaglespeaker family since before I was even born. Way back in the day, in Seattle, Rocky played basketball with my uncles, the great Sonny "Indian Superman" Mosquito, Dwayne Eaglespeaker, and Farley Eaglespeaker. They were legends, yo, knee-high socks and all.

This Black Indigenous man took in me and my li'l brother and treated us like kings. He treated my mama like the Queen she is.

This Black Indigenous man grew up across the street from a horse racing track, he dreamed that one day he would train horses.

This Black Indigenous man left everything he knew, and moved with us from Seattle to the Blackfeet Reservation in Browning, Montana, then to the Blood Reserve, across the border in Standoff, Alberta. He didn't complain, he knew it had to be done, my grandfather had passed on, and my grandma needed our help.

This Black Indigenous man stood out amongst all us Blackfoot peoples, he faced relentless discrimination and prejudice from us, and everywhere off the rez ... but, he never left.

This Black Indigenous man earned my peoples' respect, he learned our language, he helped with our ceremonies, he lived his dream of training horses. He even trained Chief Charlie Weaselhead's horses.

This Black Indigenous man kept me out of trouble, he kept me focused, he kept me from partying with the party-ers, he searched for me when I wasn't home on time, he gave me "that look" whenever I needed it, he never laid a hand on me or my brother. He raised us like a man should raise his boys, with love and understanding and a li'l bit of *"boy, you better get your ass home!"*

This Black Indigenous man is cooler than a polar bear's toenail, and when it comes to racial confrontation, he keeps his cool in a cooler. Well, except this one time, when I was a little kid, this car cut us off in a Safeway parking lot, Rocky got out to calmly speak with the driver, a white guy. I watched thru the car window. It looked like things were getting heated, then suddenly, I heard the big white guy yell "N****R". That was the first, and only, time I have seen someone get roundhouse kicked in the face, it was just like in the movies. Rocky got back in the car, cool as a cucumber, and said *"we best go before the police come"*. (well, that's how I remember it)

This Black Indigenous man left the reserve, with my mama, when his grandma passed, and his mama needed help, back in Minneapolis. Rocky and my mama have been there ever since.

This Black Indigenous man lives a mere mile from where George Floyd was killed by police, on May 25, 2020, with a knee to the back of his throat, for 8 agonizing minutes and 46 deathly seconds. George begged to breathe, he begged for his mama, he begged for his life. He was no different than the Black man who raised me.

Thank you Rocky, for making me into a man, for loving my mama all these years, like she deserves to be loved. You're my hero.

I love you ...

CONTRIBUTING AUTHORS

Annie Wesley
Dear George Floyd

Dr Dawn Karima
The Things We Forgive

Kayla Ironstar
Untitled

Kelly Tudor
His Hair Tells A Story

Deirdre Lee
Talking With My Sisters
Honey Bee Lips

Marlin Legare
The RCMP

Tammy Galinec
I Am Metis, I Am Whole, I Am One

Killa Cha'ska
50 Shades of Brown

Stephanie Big Eagle
Thunderbird Rising

Jocelyn Paul
I Am A Metis Woman

Maria Guzman
An Easy Target

Rudy Kelly
Living In Two Worlds

... and a huge thanks to the hundreds of respondents to the 5 injustice questions

MORE FROM EAGLESPEAKER PUBLISHING

NAPI CHILDREN'S BOOKS:

Napi and the Rock

Napi and the Bullberries

Napi and the Wolves

Napi and the Buffalo

Napi and the Chickadees

Napi and the Coyote

Napi and the Elk

Napi and the Gophers

Napi and the Mice

Napi: The Anthology

GRAPHIC NOVELS:

UNeducation: A Residential School Graphic Novel

Napi the Trixster: A Blackfoot Graphic Novel

UNeducation, Vol 2: The Side of Society You Don't See On TV

COLLABORATIONS:

Young Water Protectors

Mukwa & The Suitcase

The Empowerment of Eahwahewi

Descendants of Warriors

How The Earth Was Created

I Am The Opioid Crisis

My Ribbon Skirts

The Secret of the Stars

Stimtema: 13 Grandmother Moons

Teeias Goes To A Powwow

Aahksoyo'p Nootski Cookbook

... and many more at eaglespeaker.com

If you find this book captivating, please tell your friends, then find it on AMAZON.COM and leave a quick review. Your words help more than you may realize. Thanks so much.

For bulk orders, and to check out our huge selection of books by new Indigenous authors, visit **eaglespeaker.com**